More Advance Praise for
Training That Delivers Results

"This book details a breakthrough process for creating learning solutions. The mandate is clear: Learning solutions must align with an organization's business goals and provide measurable results. This book is *the* guide for how to achieve that outcome."

—Jim and Dana Robinson,
coauthors of *Performance Consulting*

"This book is much more than a *how to* because it includes the rationale behind each step that professionals require to respond to real client demands."

—Judith Hale, President,
Hale Associates, Inc.

"Dick Handshaw has written a very compelling, practical, and visual approach that links instructional design and performance consulting to help achieve business results through proactive consulting and value-add learning solutions. If you are interested in improving your company, your team, or your capability, this is one book you need to read."

—Donna J. Burrer, Senior Vice President,
Business Training, KeyBank

"For any of the learning organizations out there struggling to become a 'strategic trusted partner' to the business and deliver results that have impact, this is MUST-read book on performance consulting. Dick offers a simple and effective step-by-step model with case studies to drive home the application. You will find a piece of you and your team in every case study!"

—Heather Parks, Learning Executive and President,
New Dimensions Coaching

"*Training That Delivers Results* is a 'must have' book that delivers the results it promises and more. Dick Handshaw takes the mystery out of what it takes to create sound learning solutions to any customer's business-driven needs in the real world. Even more, he models how to 'think' like a performance consultant who can adapt, build trust, and deliver the right learning and non-learning solutions to achieve desired business goals."

—Timothy R. Brock, Ph.D., CPT, CEO,
The Institute 4 Worthy Performance LLC

"*Training That Delivers Results* sets a new standard by combining the fundamentals of performance consulting and training design with the components of organizational culture. Dick Handshaw provides a proven and comprehensive model for creating learning experiences with long-lasting value. This book is a call to action for all strategic human resource and organizational development professionals."

—Barbara L. Thornton, founder and President,
People Development Partners

TRAINING THAT DELIVERS RESULTS

Instructional Design That Aligns with Business Goals

DICK HANDSHAW

AMERICAN MANAGEMENT ASSOCIATION

New York • Atlanta • Brussels • Chicago • Mexico City • San Francisco
Shanghai • Tokyo • Toronto • Washington, D. C.

Bulk discounts available. For details visit:
www.amacombooks.org/go/specialsales
Or contact special sales:
Phone: 800-250-5308
E-mail: specialsls@amanet.org
View all the AMACOM titles at: www.amacombooks.org
American Management Association: www.amanet.org

This publication is designed to provide accurate and authoritative information in regard to the subject matter covered. It is sold with the understanding that the publisher is not engaged in rendering legal, accounting, or other professional service. If legal advice or other expert assistance is required, the services of a competent professional person should be sought.

Handshaw, Dick.
    Training that delivers results : instructional design that aligns with business goals / Dick Handshaw.
— 1 Edition.
        pages cm
    Includes bibliographical references and index.
    ISBN 978-0-8144-3403-1 — ISBN 0-8144-3403-7   1. Organizational learning.
2. Employees—Training of.   3. Performance standards.   I. Title.
    HD58.82.H367 2014
    658.3'124—dc23
                            2014005597

About ASTD
ASTD (American Society for Training & Development) is the world's largest association dedicated to the training and development profession. ASTD's members come from more than 100 countries and connect locally in more than 120 U.S. chapters and with more than 16 international partners. Members work in thousands of organizations of all sizes, in government, as independent consultants, and suppliers.
    Started in 1943, in recent years ASTD has widened the profession's focus to link learning and performance to individual and organizational results, and is a sought-after voice on critical public policy issues.

About AMA
American Management Association (www.amanet.org) is a world leader in talent development, advancing the skills of individuals to drive business success. Our mission is to support the goals of individuals and organizations through a complete range of products and services, including classroom and virtual seminars, webcasts, webinars, podcasts, conferences, corporate and government solutions, business books, and research. AMA's approach to improving performance combines experiential learning—learning through doing—with opportunities for ongoing professional growth at every step of one's career journey.

Printing number

10 9 8 7 6 5 4 3 2 1

Contents

Introduction

WHY INSTRUCTIONAL DESIGN *AND* PERFORMANCE CONSULTING?

This book helps you combine the discipline of instructional design with that of performance consulting to create a new approach to designing instruction that focuses on achieving real business results. By linking training and non-training goals to strategic business goals and tracking the impact of those solutions, we provide increased value to our organizations.

When I started my career, the ADDIE (Analyze, Design, Develop, Implement, and Evaluate) type of instructional design model was not well known or used. Today, ADDIE models are well known, but the training profession has questioned their continued value. I began practicing performance consulting along with instructional design in the mid-1990s. I am completely convinced of the value of combining the two disciplines. Both of these disciplines depend on measurement for their success. This book introduces you to the Handshaw Instructional Design Model, which combines the ADDIE approach with measurement and performance consulting to align your instructional design with business goals.

➡ Who Is This Book For?

Whether you are new to the learning profession or not, you will find useful, evidence-based practices throughout this book. I have tried to write in as straightforward a manner as possible. I have been careful to explain industry terms and jargon. Even experienced instructional designers will benefit from the case studies, stories, tools, and examples.

Managers and learning leaders who are held accountable for delivering results may find new strategies for measuring and proving results. Human resource professionals who interface with training teams will find strategies to better leverage those resources and solutions. This book also includes easy-to-follow best practices for performance consultants.

▶ How to Use the Handshaw Model

The key to using the Handshaw model successfully is flexibility. You will learn about the cost-vs.-risk rule that helps you determine which steps in the model should be used in a given situation and what resources should be spent on them. An instructional design model is not a cookbook recipe. The reason some instructional design models do not produce optimal results is the way they are used—or misused. A model, according to scientist Karl Deutsch, is a "structure of symbols and operating rules which is supposed to match a set of relevant points in an existing structure or process." The chapters in this book, each dedicated to a different phase of the model, help you use the systematic process of instructional design differently, based on the needs of each new situation.

▶ How to Use This Book

This book takes you through each phase of the Handshaw Instructional Design Model and helps you apply the process to any given situation. A graphic of the Handshaw model serves as a guide to move you from one phase to the next. Each phase ends with a transition to the next. Each chapter is written to stand on its own for review purposes or if you are only interested in certain phases. It is designed to be a practical, how-to book with lots of takeaways to apply in your work.

No theoretical process by itself can help you achieve results unless it is adopted and trusted by key stakeholders and influencers in your organization. The last chapter in the book helps you manage the change involved in adopting this model. It requires vision and persistence on the part of the individual practitioner to adopt this process. The payoff is an organization that measures success and delivers results. The process has its rewards, both measurable and intrinsic.

CHAPTER 1

A New Model for Results

*T*raining That Delivers Results aims to change learning organizations and their leaders by offering a strategic model that focuses on achieving desired business results. The strategic instructional design process described in this book produces observable, measurable, and repeatable training programs that deliver results. *Observable* means that you are able to clearly see the intended behaviors of and outcomes achieved by your performers. *Measurable* means that you are able to compare the results of your learner's performance against a predetermined standard. The system is efficient and predictable yet still offers room for flexibility and creativity.

The Handshaw Instructional Design Model applies principles of both performance improvement and instructional design to a variety of learning situations. Achieving business-focused outcomes begins by identifying both learning and nonlearning solutions to performance problems. Instructional design practiced this way doesn't *cost* time and money, it *saves* time and money.

PERFORMANCE IMPROVEMENT AND INSTRUCTIONAL DESIGN

Some people in our profession consider themselves instructional designers; others consider themselves to be performance consultants. An effective way to deliver value is by integrating the skills of both performance improvement and instructional design. Adding the steps of performance consulting from the Handshaw Instructional Design Model enables you to link learning goals to strategic business goals.

▶ A New Model

The Handshaw Instructional Design Model integrates the principles of performance improvement with those of classic instructional design (see Figure 1.1). Although many of the parts of this model are not new, the concept of combining elements of performance improvement and instructional design into one straightforward, easy-to-use model is new. If your instructional design model is not saving you time and delivering business results, then this may be an approach to consider. By identifying both learning and nonlearning solutions up front, designers are better able to spend their time and resources delivering solutions that solve the right performance challenges. I have spent more than thirty years working with my team and our clients to refine our model and its application in a wide variety of situations. The following section describes the basics for applying the model.

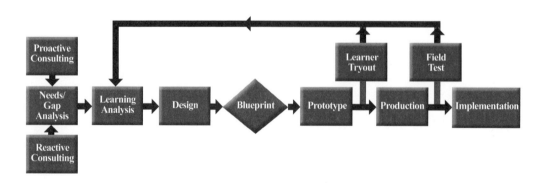

FIGURE 1.1   Handshaw Instructional Design Model

THE HANDSHAW INSTRUCTIONAL DESIGN MODEL EXPLAINED

▶ Proactive Performance Consulting

You can establish a consulting relationship with your client through *proactive performance consulting* (see Figure 1.2). The purpose of establishing this relationship is to ensure that the training you develop aligns with your client's business goals. You can develop a "trusted partner" relationship with your client by having regular proactive consulting meetings. These meetings are informal, conversational, and simple to conduct. The eight well-tested principles of the successful proactive consulting meeting are detailed in Chapter 2.

▶ Reactive Performance Consulting

Most instructional designers are accustomed to meeting with their clients to react to training requests. These meetings present an opportunity to reframe the training request in order to align the training need with the business need. The reactive consulting meetings position you to take responsibility for results and outcomes of a learning program and help you transition from training "order taker" to trusted partner. (See Figure 1.3.)

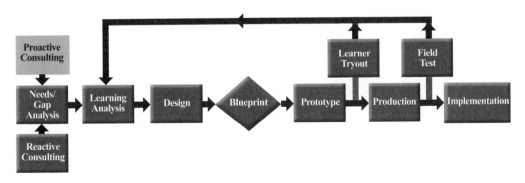

FIGURE 1.2 Proactive Performance Consulting Phase

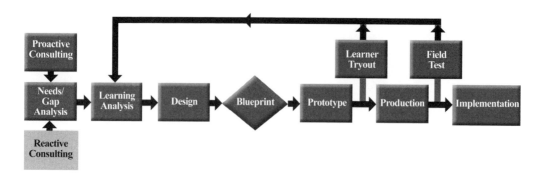

FIGURE 1.3   Reactive Performance Consulting Phase

⮞ Needs/Gap Analysis

The *gap analysis* is a frequently used type of needs analysis. It may be used after a successful proactive or reactive meeting in which appropriate learning needs have been identified. The first gap you identify is the difference between the current and the expected business outcomes. Next, determine the gap between the current performance and the performance required to achieve the business result. The exact level of performance required to close the gap is defined during the Analysis and Design phases in the model. Armed with

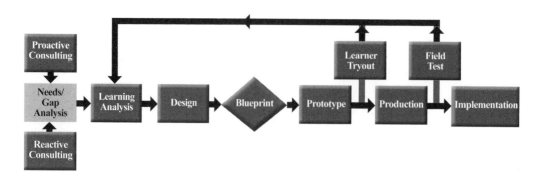

FIGURE 1.4   Needs/Gap Analysis Phase

this information, you can identify both learning and nonlearning solutions to help you and your client close both the performance and the business gaps. (See Figure 1.4.)

➧ Learning Analysis

Once you have identified the skills gap, the Learning Analysis phase begins (Figure 1.5). The first step, a *task analysis,* is essentially a snapshot of the perfect performer engaging in a work task in a way that achieves the desired business result. Developing a task analysis verified by subject matter experts (SMEs) and stakeholders before beginning training design is an essential step. It is cost effective and helps you avoid project delays and cost overruns.

There are three other types of analysis that help you make decisions later, during the Design phase. You can conduct an *audience analysis* to find out what your learners already know about the training program's content. Collecting helpful demographic information about the intended audience is also part of this analysis. The audience analysis doesn't require a lot of time and can be reused when conducting training for the same audience in the future.

Many organizations overlook the importance of culture. Culture can be

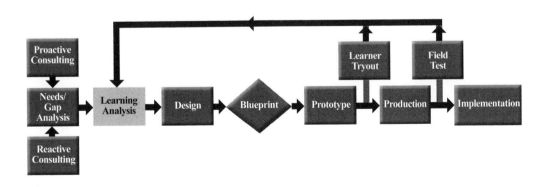

FIGURE 1.5   Learning Analysis Phase

one of the greatest enhancers or strongest barriers to a successful learning event. Conduct a *learning culture analysis* to leverage your organization's culture to impact the ultimate, lasting success of your learning design.

The last piece of analysis you should complete is called a *delivery systems analysis*. This may be more useful for outside service providers than for internal practitioners, but conducting this type of analysis might help you avoid the really embarrassing situation of specifying the use of an unpopular or poorly performing learning delivery system. A delivery systems analysis can also be revised and reused for future projects.

▶ Design

The Design phase (Figure 1.6) begins with the development of *performance objectives* (you can substitute *learning objectives* if you prefer that term). Successful selection and design of measurement instruments begins with well-written objectives. Although I am a proponent of flexibility, I don't recommend it here. You will reap the benefits of good objectives when measuring learning outcomes—for example, when you are required to measure a learner's mastery of performance objectives.

It also makes sense to select and design your testing instruments once

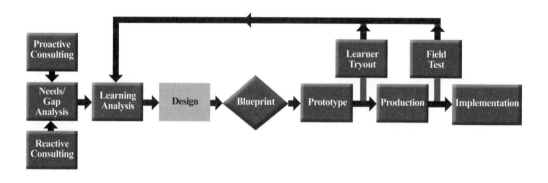

FIGURE 1.6   Design Phase

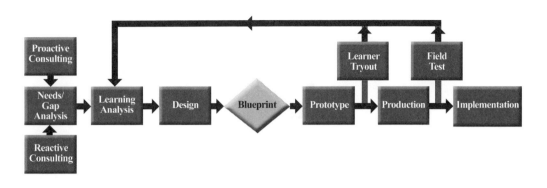

FIGURE 1.7   Blueprint Phase

you have agreed upon objectives. When designing for results, you should limit your test design to criterion-referenced tests (CRTs) only. The criteria you reference in this case are the performance objectives. The payback for following these steps will be apparent when you define your instructional strategy. You can eliminate misunderstandings by defining a measurement strategy before you try to select an instructional strategy.

➤ Blueprint

You won't find the *blueprint meeting* in any traditional instructional design model such as ADDIE (Analysis, Design, Develop, Implement, and Evaluate). This tool is essential to the development of a performance partnership with your clients. A blueprint meeting is a forum that allows you to present your measurement strategy and instructional strategy to your stakeholders, subject matter experts, and others on the design team. The meeting can be held in person or virtually and is ideal for answering questions, clarifying misunderstandings, and gaining consensus. If you really want to be a trusted partner, invest two or three hours in this meeting. (See Figure 1.7.)

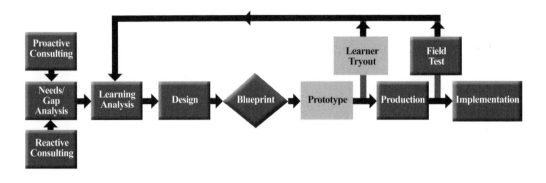

FIGURE 1.8   Prototype and Learner Tryout Phases

➧ Prototype and Learner Tryout

Another useful tool for preventing "do-overs" and gaining consensus as a trusted partner is the simple step of developing and testing a *prototype*. First, select a training module for your prototype that is a fair representation of your measurement and instructional strategies. Then, before you go too far in developing the rest of the course, test your prototype with a small group of sample learners in a *learner tryout*. Use this structured test to yield valuable data for verifying your chosen strategies. You may discover differences of opinion with your subject matter experts or even among designers on your own team. I've found that observing sample learners during a learner tryout always uncovers the correct approach. The feedback loops in the model allow you to go back and revise the analysis and subsequent design steps. (See Figure 1.8.)

➧ Production and Field Test

The Production phase is the largest and costliest of all the phases in the model (see Figure 1.9). It involves development of content and testing instruments. Because this phase is so time consuming, it is important to ensure that the other phases are done correctly in order to avoid rework.

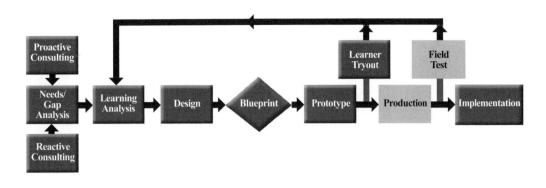

FIGURE 1.9   Production and Field Test Phases

The evaluation carried out in this phase is called a *field test* (some of our clients prefer the term *pilot test*). Whatever label you use, you need to observe sample learners as they test the entire learning solution under the exact conditions they will experience during implementation. Testing your course with a controlled audience provides a measure of reassurance to you and your client that the rollout will go smoothly. This is a good feeling to have if your course is going to be released to a large audience in a global organization.

⯈ Implementation

If you've carefully followed the recommended steps in the model, the Implementation phase should proceed according to plan (Figure 1.10). But sometimes well-designed and -executed learning programs fail due to poor implementation, despite the use of a detailed implementation plan. Why would this happen? Look for answers in your audience and learning culture analyses. These documents guide you in designing your implementation plan. Your implementation plan also should include change management plans, timelines, resources, logistics, and measurement of business impact and return on investment (ROI).

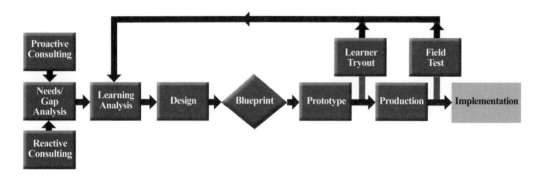

FIGURE 1.10   Implementation Phase

ONE DESIGNER'S FIRST CLIENT

The following case study illustrates how even a new learning practitioner can combine the practice of performance improvement and instructional design to solve a performance problem and achieve real business results. Ken, the instructional designer in this case study, is a recent graduate of a master's program in Instructional Systems Technology. The client request discussed in this narrative came about three months after Ken began work for a regional bank.

▶ The Request

Ken was getting comfortable with his new job when he was contacted by Bill. Bill was responsible for an insurance product offered along with auto loans that would pay off the auto loan note in the case of the death or disability of the borrower. Revenue was down for this product, and Bill was concerned because fee income was becoming an increasingly important part of the bank's revenue stream. Bill approached Ken and asked him to produce some training on product knowledge. He handed Ken a PowerPoint file from another bank's training program and asked Ken to develop both instructor-led training and e-learning.

▶ The Analysis

Having been schooled in instructional systems design, Ken asked to meet with Bill to develop task and audience analyses. Bill was polite and gracious, but he informed Ken that a two-day meeting of his entire team was scheduled to occur in about a month and the training had to be ready by then. Bill said he wanted to devote up to half of that time to training. Bill again insisted that his script be repurposed as an instructor-led event for the meeting. He also emphasized that he wanted an online version prepared for anyone who couldn't attend the meeting or anyone needing a refresher after the meeting.

Being new to the corporate world, Ken faced a dilemma. He had been taught the value of analysis, so he wasn't prepared for a client who didn't understand why analysis was important even with a tight deadline. Still, he did the only thing he could do. He took the script and promised to have everything ready on time.

Later that afternoon, Ken dropped by Bill's office with a few technical questions on the model script. While he was in Bill's office, Ken asked Bill if he could talk to some of the people who were having difficulty with the product so that he could better understand the problem. Bill told Ken there was no time to gather information, but he did offer to take Ken's questions with him on a trip he had previously scheduled to visit some of the bank's branches. Ken quickly crafted six questions about product knowledge based on what he knew from his review of the PowerPoint script and gave them to Bill.

When Bill returned from his trip a few days later, Ken asked Bill how the trip had gone. He was especially interested in the answers to the questions Bill had taken with him.

"Those questions you gave me were just questions about product knowledge," Bill commented.

"That's right," said Ken. "So, how did they do?"

"Well, they did pretty well. Almost everybody I asked knew the answers to all six of your questions."

Bill had to admit that everyone he questioned had adequate product knowledge. Ken saw this as an opening to make a point.

"So, Bill," Ken said, "do you still think spending all your training time on product knowledge is what you want me to do?"

For the first time, Bill looked a little perturbed, but he kept his patience and asked, "Well, what do you think?"

This was the turning point in the relationship. Ken had just crossed the line from being an order taker to becoming a trusted partner. He knew his next question was the most important one of his new career.

"Bill, can you tell me, from a business perspective, what you need to accomplish? What is your business goal?"

Bill's demeanor changed completely. He shared with Ken that for the last three months, only 30 percent of auto loans had any insurance products connected with them. His target was to have insurance products connected to 60 percent of all auto loans. Ken immediately recognized that this information was the basis for a learning and performance goal. He asked Bill if they could schedule a meeting the next day to discuss some other options. This time, Bill quickly agreed.

While answering questions about how the performers should go about presenting the insurance product to potential auto loan customers, Bill mentioned a key piece of information. He said that most lending officers admitted that they never or rarely mentioned the insurance product when closing an auto loan. Many lending officers said that they just didn't have time. Some said they didn't really know when the product was good for their customers, and some said they didn't like to mention the insurance product because many customers complained that it cost too much money. Some said they just liked being bankers and didn't want to feel like insurance salespeople. Now our designer had some data that he could use to solve Bill's problem.

With just a little bit of data, the solution became clear. Ken got permission to speak with some of the top performers who were achieving higher sales of the insurance products so he could produce a high-level task analysis of a sales process that was working. The gaps in performance were clear:

- Successful performers mentioned the insurance product early in their overall loan closing process. Most of the loan officers never mentioned the insurance products at all.

- Successful performers used a series of questions to qualify their loan customers to identify them as good candidates for the insurance products. Most of the loan officers never mentioned the insurance products at all.

- Successful performers were able to relate stories of past customers who had benefitted from the purchase of the insurance products. Most of the loan officers never mentioned the insurance products at all.

- Successful performers saw customer objections, especially to price, as buying signals and had a strategy for handling these objections. Most of the loan officers never mentioned the insurance products at all.

- Finally, successful performers never mentioned lack of product knowledge as a barrier in selling the insurance products.

➡ The Proposal

Based on the identified performance gaps and the additional analysis, Ken proposed the following solution:

1. Begin the instructor-led session with real stories of customers who benefitted from having purchased the insurance products. This information was easy to gather from product files.

2. Show video role plays of the successful loan closing process highlighting the presentation, qualifying, and objection handling for the insurance products. Include some role plays of common mistakes.

3. Conduct sample role plays with as many participants as possible, inviting feedback from other participants.

4. Conduct additional role plays handling different types of customer objections.

5. Include some drill and practice on product knowledge (just to keep Bill happy). Design and provide a job aid for product knowledge.

⬥ The Solution

Bill accepted the entire proposal. Ironically, the only thing he actually questioned was the need for the last component, concerning product knowledge. Ken convinced Bill to keep this point mostly for the value of the job aid and to further increase the confidence level of the participants. Bill was convinced that increasing the confidence level of the participants was likely to have the most significant impact on achieving his business goal of a 60 percent close rate. The instructor-led component, including sample videos and other written materials, was completed in the remaining three and a half weeks before the meeting, and all of the training was completed in the first full day of the two-day meeting.

The first class was attended by thirty-five participants. By splitting participants into different rooms, almost everyone was able to participate in a live role-play situation. Everyone received feedback on the role play based on a checklist, which was based on the task analysis and the objectives. Bill was able to identify the successful performers in the group, and he was also able to single out those who needed additional coaching.

◆ The Results

Three months after the meeting, 60 percent of all loans had insurance products connected to the loan. That rate was double the 30 percent rate for each of the three months prior to the meeting. Bill was so happy that he told everyone in the bank about his success and about his new strategic business partner.

◆ And Now, the Rest of the Story . . .

The preceding case study narrative was mostly true, except the young designer's name was not Ken. His real name was Dick, and the story recalls my experience as a newly minted instructional designer in 1979. But, as they say, the more things change, the more they stay the same. The PowerPoint script was actually a script from a sound-slide presentation. As a historical note, a sound-slide presentation is a 1970s version of today's PowerPoint that contained words, graphics, and a sound track read by a narrator.

How would the prospects for designing an effective learning program have been any different if you had received an e-mail from a contemporary like Bill with a PowerPoint file attached? Learning professionals call this kind of training program "check-in-a-box" training—that is, performing a learning activity without an expectation of any measurable results.

In my early career example, the client achieved his business goal and I met the tight, four-week deadline without spending much money. I didn't go through a long, complicated process. I didn't employ a complicated instructional design model. I didn't even know there were such things as performance improvement models. What I did was reframe my client's request to focus on business outcomes rather than training activities. I got permission to conduct a little more analysis. My client identified the business gap for me, and together we identified the performance gap. With the help of his best performers, we identified the best practices, analyzed the task, and developed measurement and instructional strategies to achieve the performance goal. Achieving the performance goal in turn achieved the business goal.

WHAT DO TODAY'S LEARNING PROFESSIONALS NEED?

Today's learning professionals are faced with more challenges than ever before. Not only are they expected to work with clients as expert instructional designers, they are also expected to be training facilitators, adept in the use of different e-learning authoring tools and learning management systems (LMSs). It's clearly unreasonable to expect these diverse talents to exist in one person.

Still, if you are part of a small learning team, it's inevitable that you will be expected to be adept at a variety of skills. For some people, this expectation offers a good opportunity to discover their strengths and weaknesses. Instructional design is definitely a team sport. It is a far better career strategy to improve as much as you can in your areas of strength and rely on your team members to make up for your weaknesses. How well you engage with your team determines your success as a learning professional.

If you are serious about this profession, a master's degree in Instructional Systems Technology or a related field will open many doors, but you won't find many undergraduate programs that prepare you to be a learning professional in the corporate world. A degree and experience in public education are an excellent background for entering the corporate learning field.

Ongoing professional development is also important for learning professionals. While many of the design principles remain the same, their application (especially with constantly evolving technology) is ever changing. You can keep up with the field by attending conferences or meetings that base their topics on research and evidence-based practices. Refer to the Appendix for a short list of the leading professional associations.

Finally, learning professionals today need to be responsible for business results. Training departments are often the first place organizations cut costs. The only way to change this dynamic is to partner with your organization to achieve business goals. Being a training order taker who accepts only the responsibility to complete a required number of training programs is not a partnering relationship that provides value to your client or organization.

THE FIRST PHASE . . .

Chapter 2 helps you build a trusted partner relationship with your clients. You will learn how to reframe some training requests to identify business goals and subsequently define training goals that help achieve the business goals. You will be able to identify other solutions to the results you seek besides just training solutions. You will also be able to take a proactive approach to help you keep close to your clients and establish your consulting relationship before your client comes to you with a request.

CHAPTER 2

Performance Consulting

The Handshaw Instructional Design Model allows you to take either a proactive or a reactive consulting approach with your client (see Figure 2.1). Regardless of your approach, using the model means you will be developing a strategic partnering relationship with your clients that puts both of you on the road to achieving desired business results.

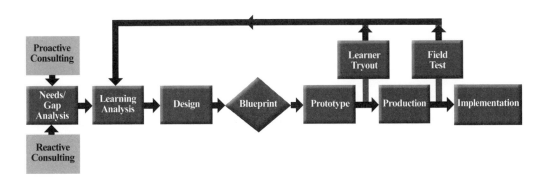

FIGURE 2.1 Handshaw Instructional Design Model: Proactive and Reactive Consulting

THE NEED FOR RELATIONSHIPS

In your role as an internal practitioner or an external consultant, building a network and maintaining a relationship with your clients, subject matter experts, team members, and partners is one of the most important responsibilities of a training professional.

The most common complaint I hear from training professionals is that they don't like being viewed as order takers for training activities. It's a legitimate complaint and certainly frustrating. How can you, as an individual instructional designer, consultant, or manager, change this existing perception in your organization? It starts with you and your relationship with your clients. New organizational structures rarely are capable of changing the way clients view learning organizations. Empower yourself to practice and manage your relationship using performance consulting to build the necessary trust with your clients. We all know of learning organizations that keep doing the same things over and over, producing the same results with their learning programs. At times, a learning leader may decide to bring in a new model to promote change in the learning organization when that change does not impact the enterprise as a whole. Assess your skills and develop a plan to get your seat at the table so you can impact your individual client relationships.

▶ The True Client

Relationship building with your clients begins in two ways. When you respond to a request, you are using the *reactive* performance consulting approach. When you initiate a consulting meeting, you are using the *proactive* performance consulting approach. Both approaches require that you first identify your *true client*.

The true client for any performance improvement effort is the owner of the line of business that is experiencing the performance problem. This person knows the current business goal, the internal and external barriers, and the strongest and weakest performers. The true client is the only person who can answer the questions you will be asking as you conduct reactive and proactive consulting meetings. This person can make the decisions that will ultimately affect the final business results.

REACTIVE PERFORMANCE CONSULTING

You are probably already familiar with the reactive consulting approach if clients e-mail or call you with requests for you to develop training. They probably tell you what they want, how they want it delivered, and how long they want it to take. You may or may not be comfortable with this approach, but you are probably used to it.

Why don't your clients listen to your advice as a learning or performance consultant? Part of the problem is human nature. People are not always willing to take advice. I found some guidance on this situation from a somewhat unlikely source—a Chinese fortune cookie. My fortune said, "People are not persuaded by what we say but rather by what they understand." The challenge for instructional designers is: How do we make people understand our recommendation and why it is good for them?

You can solve this problem by applying the principles of *reframing* training requests. I was introduced to this concept in the mid-1990s. I was attending a meeting with a client who had just taken a new job as director of training. He told his new team of 125 people, "The training department here is doing a great job developing training, but you're developing too much training." I was not the only one puzzled by his statement. The point my client was trying to make is that not all performance problems can be solved by training. There are times when you suspect that training may not solve your client's entire problem. This is an opportunity for you to reframe the request.

The Reactive Performance Consulting phase is a good place to begin using the Handshaw Instructional Design Model (Figure 2.2). Once you have had

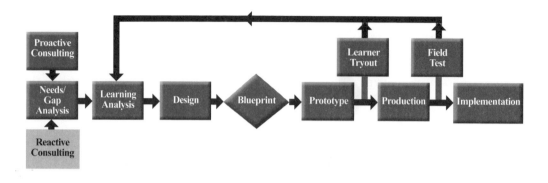

FIGURE 2.2   Handshaw Instructional Design Model: Reactive Consulting

some success with proactive consulting, you will have less need for the reactive approach, but reframing meetings will always be part of your job, whether you like it or not. The reactive approach is challenging but very rewarding once you get used to it.

When you say "no" to a client who has come to you with a training request, whether it is valid or not, you risk damaging your trusted relationship. In order to be seen as a trusted partner, you need to acknowledge the client's concern every time he or she approaches you with a training request. Instead of saying "no," start by acknowledging the client's concern. Try to shift the conversation to outcomes and business results and away from activities.

A successful result of this conversation should be agreement between you and your client on a shared business goal. The goal should be stated more in terms of outcomes and results than activities. The goal of your reframing meeting should be to gain permission from the client to collect analysis data to help you make an informed decision on how to proceed. Schedule a follow-up meeting to share your findings, and let your data speak for itself.

Here are eight principles for conducting a successful reframing meeting:

1. Start with the mindset of the client.

2. Acknowledge the client's concern.

3. Ask open-ended questions.

4. Focus on shared business goals and results.

5. Restate and summarize often.

6. Let the data speak for itself.

7. Continually engage the client.

8. Push back when the client's preferred action is not helpful.

To watch a video role play demonstration of a successful reactive consulting meeting, go to www.dhandshaw.com and click on the Resources tab.

PROACTIVE PERFORMANCE CONSULTING

If you are tired of always having to reframe the request and trying to make your point, there is a better way. With the proactive consulting approach, you can build a strategic partnering relationship by approaching your client when there is no current request or pressing issue. You simply want to understand your client's business, the goals, and the things that keep your client awake at night. Once you learn to truly listen and "walk in your client's shoes," you begin to bridge your own gap from order taker to strategic partner.

When you try using reactive performance consulting, you will discover that reframing a training request is a skill that requires practice. Once you learn to leverage your proactive consulting skills, you will have less need for your reframing skills. The idea of proactive consulting is to create a trusted, consulting relationship before there is a request for training. Waiting until your client is pressed for time, under stress, and already convinced he or she has the answer to a performance problem is not the time to begin building the consulting relationship. In this situation, you can try reframing or you may be forced to settle for just taking the order. You have to remember to pick your battles.

In order to participate on a strategic level, you have to be proactive. That means you should seek to understand your client's business, including his or her pains and opportunities, before a specific initiative or project arises. Building trust among individuals takes time, especially when there are risks at stake. It's not something you can put on a project schedule or assign a convenient due date. It's an investment you make over time, and it does pay off. In their latest book, *Performance Consulting,* second edition, Jim and Dana Robinson explain that the purpose of the proactive discussion is "to deepen your knowledge of your client's business and to strengthen your relationship with your client. But you also have your antennae up to identify opportunities where you might add value when you have not been asked to be part of the project."

Mastering the skill of proactive consulting resolves most of your complaints about being seen strictly as an order taker and having to use valuable corporate resources developing learning solutions that you know add little value. Beginning a methodical process of proactive consulting positions you to be invited into opportunities earlier in the process. It also gives you access to more information. You will have a greater and more informed voice in identifying solutions to problems, whether they are learning solutions or other types of solutions.

Beginning with the Proactive Performance Consulting phase gives you more lead time, gives you more client buy-in, and helps you identify the correct business and performance goals. (See Figure 2.3.)

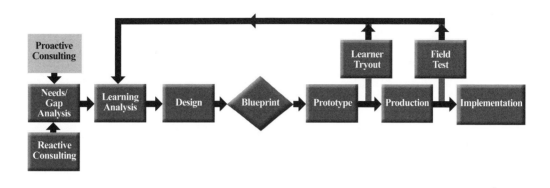

FIGURE 2.3   Handshaw Instructional Design Model: Proactive Consulting

The proactive consulting meeting is easier to conduct than the reframing meeting. You may be meeting with an existing client, or your client may be new to you. If you already have a personal relationship with this person, that just makes your job easier. If not, you need to find some way to relate on a personal level. You can't gain someone's trust unless you are willing to put a little of yourself and a personal commitment into the relationship. Find something to talk about on a personal level—your kids, hobbies, where you live, anything. Let me add a word of caution here. If your client just wants to get down to business, jump right in. Hold the small talk until later. You have to be sensitive about when to get personal and when to stick to business.

The purpose of the proactive consulting meeting is for you to assess the nature and condition of your client's business. You need to speak with the true client, the person who really is responsible for the success or failure of that line of business. As you explore the nature of the client's business, you will uncover both wants and needs. To help identify strategic business needs in order to focus on outcomes rather than activities, you can ask the same magic question you asked in the reframing meeting: What is your business goal? That's all it takes.

Once you have defined a business goal, you should immediately determine how to measure the business goal. Borrowing again from the reframing meeting, restating and summarizing your client's main statements is a powerful tool to verify understanding, for both you and your client. Avoid offering your thoughts or opinions. I know this is difficult, but it is far better to let the client's own data speak for you. If you lack data, ask for permission and time to collect it. In closing the meeting, agree upon a regular schedule for having proactive consulting meetings. You can determine whether you want to have them monthly or every other month or quarterly. Meeting on a regular schedule keeps you abreast of new initiatives before they have a chance to take off without you.

As with the reframing meeting, there are eight principles to help you conduct a successful proactive consulting meeting:

1. Develop a personal relationship.

2. Assess the nature and condition of the business.

3. Separate needs from wants.

4. Focus on shared business goals and results.

5. Set usable metrics for the business goals.

6. Restate and summarize often.

7. Let the data speak for itself.

8. Set a time for the next meeting or the next step.

When you are reacting to a client request in a reactive consulting meeting, it is difficult to be prepared with a list of questions to ask. Proactive consulting meetings are easier to conduct if you bring a prepared list of questions with you. The following ten questions are taken from Jim and Dana Robinson's book *Performance Consulting*:

1. What is a major business goal for you and your business unit for the next twelve months?

2. Why is this goal important at this time? What are the driving forces behind this goal?

3. What indicators are you using to measure this goal? What are the current results relative to these metrics?

4. What strategies are you using to accomplish this goal?

5. What factors outside our organization are going to challenge goal achievement? What factors inside our organization will encourage success?

6. What factors inside our organization will challenge achievement of the goal? What factors in our organization now encourage our success?

7. Within your business unit, what employee group(s) will most directly contribute to the achievement of this goal through their day-to-day performance?

8. Considering the business goal and challenges you are facing, what must employees in this business unit do more, better, or differently to support this goal? Are there any employees currently achieving desired results? If yes, what are they doing differently?

9. What are employees typically doing now in their day-to-day work? What are the major gaps, if any, between what you need employees to do and what they are typically doing now?

10. What barriers, if any, challenge employees to perform as you need them to?

These ten questions are intended to aid you in your conversation as you apply the eight principles of proactive consulting. They are not intended to be a script for your entire conversation. You probably won't use all of them in every meeting. You probably will not use them in their exact order. As you gain experience, you will develop some favorite go-to questions. The only way you get better at conducting these meetings is through practice.

▶ Feedback

Feedback is an important tool in helping you learn performance consulting skills. Ask a colleague to sit in on your first few meetings to give you feedback on how well you applied the eight principles. As an example, the one key principle that many novice performance consultants often fail to complete in both types of meetings is asking for the business goal. You will not achieve the desired outcome from this meeting without identifying the business goal. Your colleague, acting as your coach, will make you aware of this kind of omission. You can also serve the same function by providing feedback for your colleague when he or she is conducting a performance consulting meeting. Either way, you both learn more and become good performance consultants more quickly.

To watch a video role-play demonstration of a successful proactive consulting meeting, go to www.dhandshaw.com and click on the Resources tab.

THE NEXT PHASE . . .

You have learned how to collect valuable information by conducting either the proactive or the reactive consulting meeting with your client. The purpose of these meetings is to agree to spend time gathering more information. In the next phase you will learn how to use the new data you gathered to complete a Gaps Map. The Gaps Map helps you discover the complicated relationships between performance and business results. The results of this process will lead you and your client to a complete solution, not just a training solution.

CHAPTER 3

Closing the Performance Gap

The results of the proactive or reactive consulting meetings covered in Chapter 2 determine your next step in using the model. If you and your client have identified a clear business need and agree to collect additional analysis data, you may opt to continue to the Needs/Gap Analysis phase (Figure 3.1). If you get too much pushback from your client, you may decide to skip the Needs/Gap Analysis phase. Remember, this model is flexible and should be used differently to conform to each situation.

Regardless of your starting point, this chapter introduces a powerful tool called the Gaps Map (developed by performance consulting experts Jim and Dana Robinson). The Gaps Map allows you to incorporate performance

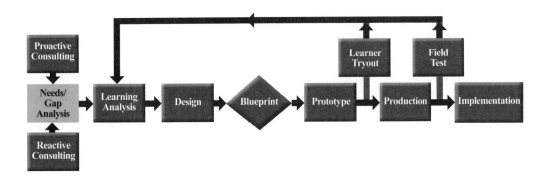

FIGURE 3.1 Handshaw Instructional Design Model: Needs/Gap Analysis

improvement into your instructional design. This process ensures that your designs achieve your client's business goals by helping you identify the root cause of a performance issue *before* you design solutions. The Gaps Map approach also guides you to design solutions that consider the full range of learning and nonlearning solutions.

THE NEEDS HIERARCHY

Before using the Gaps Map tool, you'll need a solid understanding of what performance gurus Jim and Dana Robinson call the Needs Hierarchy (Figure 3.2).

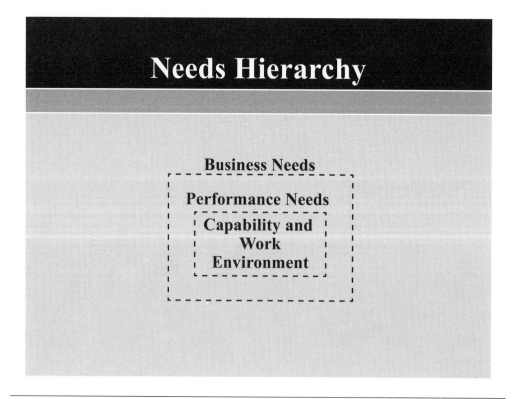

FIGURE 3.2   The Needs Hierarchy

At the top of the hierarchy is the client *business need*. The second level, or *performance need,* is the level of performance required to achieve the business goal. The third level of need, the *capability and work environment need,* focuses on other factors that impact performance (for example, learner skills and knowledge, staff shortages, or poor information systems). It's easy to understand why the Needs Hierarchy (explained in more detail in the following sections) offers a basis for understanding the Gaps Map.

▶ Business Need

Business goals must be strategic and measurable. Most business goals are connected to revenue or profit margins. You need to speak to the true client or owner of the line of business in order to identify these goals and the means to measure them. As an instructional designer, you may often be given an overall performance goal, but you have no assurance that this performance, once achieved, will result in your client achieving the business goal. The Gaps Map plays a critical role, and this is why it is so important that you use your client's own data.

▶ Performance Needs

The performance need describes the performance that your workforce should accomplish in order to achieve the business goal. If you don't correctly identify the exact performance required, you may create expensive and well-received training programs; you may even have a workforce that does what you taught them, but your client will fall short of achieving the desired business goal.

▶ Capability and Work Environment Needs

The capability need describes whether the workforce has the skills and knowledge required to succeed at the performance goal. In order for the entire process to work, you have to be sure that learning or performance goals are achievable and measurable. If you are applying a task-based approach with measurable objectives, you can almost guarantee that your performers will have the skills and knowledge required to achieve the desired performance goal.

The work environment includes anything other than skills and knowledge that can impact performers' capability of completing a task. Work environment can be a barrier to or an enhancer of achieving the performance goal. You will be able to influence changes in the work environment to enhance performers' ability to achieve both performance and business goals.

THE GAPS MAP

The Gaps Map is a tool that allows you to compare the current state of a business or process with a future desired state. With this information in hand, you can compare the two states and determine the exact performance gap. This process requires the use of precise questioning techniques and specific language for the current and desired states, such as using the words *should, is,* and *cause* to construct strategic questions.

Figure 3.3 offers three examples of measurable business needs. Use *should* statements to define the desired state and *is* statements to define the current state of the business. There are *should* and *is* statements for each of the three different business needs.

▶ Business Goals

Figure 3.3 demonstrates how the graphic representation of business goals clearly highlights the gap between the intended business results (*should*) and the actual business results (*is*).

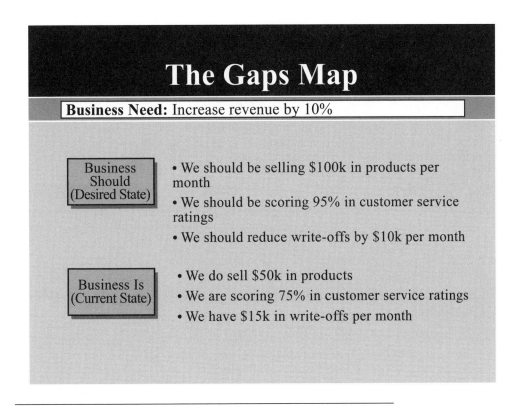

The Gaps Map

Business Need: Increase revenue by 10%

Business Should (Desired State)
- We should be selling $100k in products per month
- We should be scoring 95% in customer service ratings
- We should reduce write-offs by $10k per month

Business Is (Current State)
- We do sell $50k in products
- We are scoring 75% in customer service ratings
- We have $15k in write-offs per month

FIGURE 3.3   Business *Should*/*Is* Statements

▶ Performance Goals

Identifying performance gaps is the key to designing solutions that solve the right problems. You actually began this process in Chapter 1 when you got permission to gather more data during your proactive or reactive consulting meetings. The Gaps Map lets you apply and process the analysis data. First, you identify the performance problem underlying the current business results—the *is*. Then you compare the current state to the performance level your client's data indicates *should* deliver the expected business results. See Figure 3.4 for a typical organizational example of this *should* and *is* performance relationship.

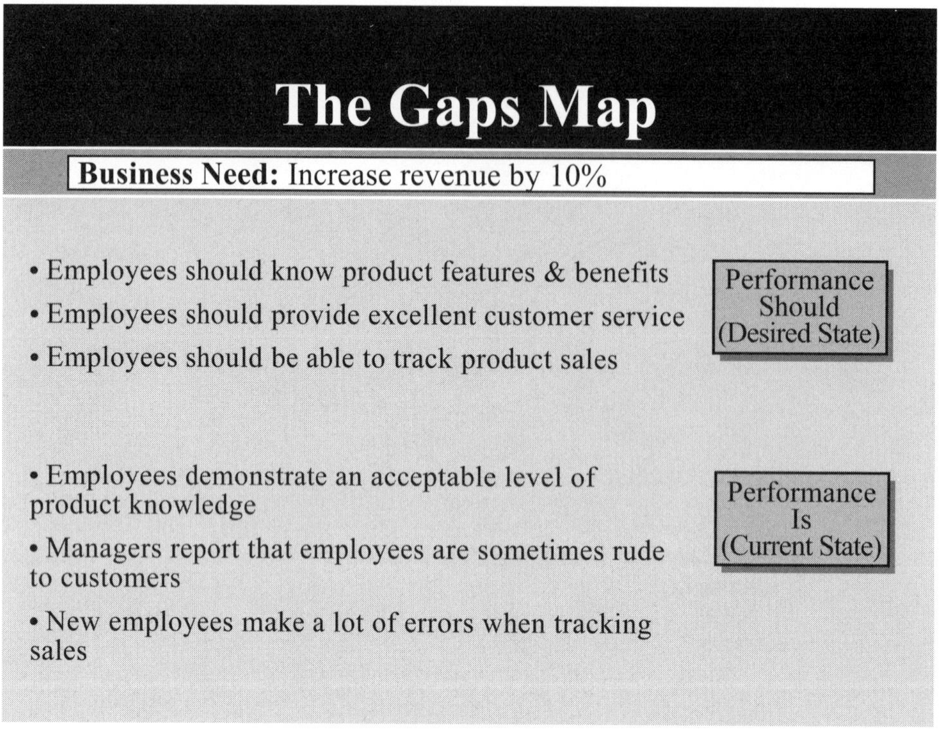

The Gaps Map

Business Need: Increase revenue by 10%

• Employees should know product features & benefits
• Employees should provide excellent customer service
• Employees should be able to track product sales

> Performance
> Should
> (Desired State)

• Employees demonstrate an acceptable level of product knowledge

• Managers report that employees are sometimes rude to customers

• New employees make a lot of errors when tracking sales

> Performance
> Is
> (Current State)

FIGURE 3.4 Performance *Should/Is* Relationship

▶ The Gaps Map Explained

Figure 3.5 is a full graphic representation of the Gaps Map. Notice that the map is divided into three sections, with the top third devoted to the *business and performance gaps,* the middle section focused on *causes,* and the bottom section labeled *solutions.* The Gaps Map can be effective only if you follow the prescribed process. First, determine the business and performance gaps, then look for causes, and, last, create solutions. Avoid jumping to solutions until your process and your data take you deliberately to a set of solutions that will deliver the desired results. Trust the process.

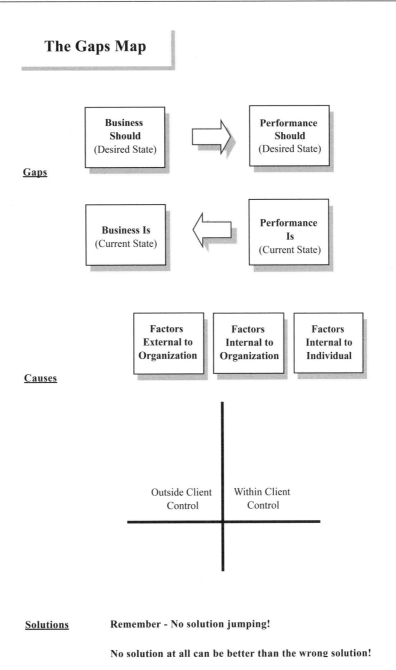

FIGURE 3.5   The Gaps Map

▶ Identify Business and Performance Gaps

You can see in Figure 3.5 that the top portion of the map is divided into the desired, or *should,* state in the top two boxes and the current, or *is,* state shown in the two boxes below them. You can begin by asking your client, "What is the current business result?" From there you can move to the desired business goal, or you can probe for the current performance that is causing the current business results. The order in which you ask the questions is up to you. You will have better success asking questions about the desired business performance if you identify the desired business goal first. It is important to understand that the desired business goal must dictate the desired performance and not the other way around. This is a key concept of the gaps portion of the model. You can see by the positioning of the two left and right arrows on the map that the business goal drives the desired performance and the current performance drives the current results.

▶ Determine Root Causes

As illustrated by the "Factors" boxes in Figure 3.5, root causes are the factors that create business and performance gaps. Your next step in using the Gaps Map, after identifying the business and performance gaps, is to analyze the potential external and internal causal factors and then identify solutions:

- **Factors external to the organization:** Identifies factors such as competition, the economy, and change in consumer tastes, which stand in the way of the desired performance. For example, if sales are slipping, an organization may assume that additional training will reverse the trend. However, your investigation may reveal that competitors are offering cheaper and better products with better customer service. In this case, training clearly is not the right or only solution.

- **Factors internal to the organization:** Identifies factors such as inadequate information systems, outdated equipment, or other work environment issues impacting performance. For example, if a sales team's performance is being impacted by outdated information, the problem might be incompatible product databases preventing access to the data or an internal information distribution problem.

- **Factors internal to the individual:** Defines whether employees have the right skills and abilities as well as the motivation to perform at the highest level. For example, a performer may be properly trained but lack motivation due to incentives such as pay increases or promotions. Determining these factors may be complex and require collecting data from a full range of top performers to poor performers.

- **Solution identification:** The last portion of the Gaps Map is reserved for the proposed solutions. Perhaps the solution involves changes or improvements in more than one area—upgrading equipment, changing incentive packages, or changing organizational processes. You may even find your client's initial training request among the proposed solutions!

PUTTING THE GAPS MAP TO WORK

In this example, our instructional designer, Jackie, works for a regional bank involved with every aspect of consumer and commercial banking. The bank is well established in the region and has five hundred branches. Jackie received a call from Tom, the senior vice president of human resources (HR). Jackie has worked with Tom for three years. Tom has asked her to join him in a meeting with Kelly, the bank's director of training. The subject of the meeting is to discuss a need for product knowledge training on the bank's growing number of consumer banking products.

In preparation for the meeting, Jackie visited the bank's website to review the current products. She noticed a few new products and several updates to many existing products. Since she is reacting to a request, this is about all the preparation she can do. She is ready for her meeting.

▶ 1. The Reframing Meeting

Tom was excited to tell Jackie about his idea to develop training for the growing number of the bank's products. For the first few minutes of the meeting she listened, asking questions only to clarify Tom's plans. Once he got all his ideas on the table, she went to work. She started with a pivotal question: "Tom, to get a better understanding for solving your problem, can you tell the underlying business goal that is driving your request?"

Tom paused for a minute and then answered, "Retail sales were flat last year, and this year, we really need a 10 percent increase in new accounts. So I've been asked by the head of the consumer bank to provide training on the growing number of products we are offering. It's getting difficult for even our experienced employees to keep up, and the newer ones are really overwhelmed."

Jackie acknowledged that the sheer number of products could be overwhelming. She had seen that for herself when she visited the bank's website. Then she looked at Kelly and Tom and asked if there was anything else they could think of that might be making it difficult for customer service representatives to sell new or existing products. Kelly added that the new-hire training programs were going well and that all new hires were required to achieve a score of 80 percent or higher. Tom added that he really wasn't sure if there were any other causes for the shortfall in new accounts. That's when Jackie asked for a meeting with the executive vice president of the consumer bank. Tom hesitated a bit, and Kelly looked at him with anticipation. Tom answered, "You know, if we're going to get to the bottom of this, that's exactly what we need to do. I'll see if I can arrange a meeting."

◆ 2. The Reframing Meeting Continued

As promised, Tom scheduled a meeting with Leslie, the executive vice president (EVP) of the consumer bank. Jackie started this meeting the same way she started the first meeting. She asked Tom to introduce his concept for developing training on the portfolio of consumer products. Kelly and Leslie agreed with Tom that his training idea sounded good. Then Jackie repeated the business goal that she had received from Tom, to make sure that Leslie was in agreement. Not only was Leslie in agreement, but she emphasized the importance of showing at least a 10 percent improvement over last year. They had spent last year revising and updating the consumer products, and this was the year they needed to see results from that work.

Jackie asked everyone in the room if they thought confusion over product knowledge was a key reason sales had remained flat for the past year. This question really got Leslie's attention. She had to admit that she was not sure how much a lack of product knowledge contributed to a flat sales effort or even if there truly was a lack of product knowledge among her staff. This was the opportunity Jackie had been looking for. She asked Leslie whom they should go to for answers to those questions. Leslie quickly wrote out a list of some regional executives and branch managers who could help. She promised Jackie she would contact each of them and let them know they needed to talk to her. The meeting ended quickly. Jackie was ready to begin her next step, data collection.

◆ 3. Data Collection

Jackie had two weeks to contact three regional execs and six branch managers. It may have seemed like a long time to Leslie, but Jackie knew she had to get busy. Because she was not looking for a simple yes/no answer, she knew she had to talk to these experts by phone or in person. She was lucky enough to speak to all nine people and gathered the following data points:

- Although there are a lot of existing consumer products—and new ones on the way—every branch has access to online product information.

- It really isn't feasible for branch personnel to memorize features and benefits for every product. Experienced people know the most commonly used products quite well, but they often refer to the online product information for less-used products.

- The updated product mix definitely positions the bank to have a better fit between products and customer needs. This should help in selling and opening new accounts as well as with overall customer satisfaction.

- There are certain times during each day and week that traffic in the bank is extremely heavy and lines tend to get long. Branch personnel are forced to abandon any efforts toward making referrals or selling new accounts when lines are long. This really forces them to miss most of the selling opportunities at a time when the largest number of future prospects is in the branch.

- The current instructor-led training on product knowledge takes too long and keeps branch personnel out of the bank at the very times when they are needed to keep up with the already inadequate staffing levels. We need a better way to conduct this training.

- Just having product knowledge available, either online or by memory, isn't enough to complete a referral or a sale. The best performers in each of the branches ask qualifying questions and recommend products based on need. They are able to tie product benefits to perceived need.

- Branch managers want shorter training classes with better results.

Now Jackie is faced with the task of what to do with the information she has gathered. She begins by trying to organize the data into a Gaps Map.

▶ 4. Preparing the Gaps Map

Jackie has a business goal, current business performance, and some good data about what is going on in the branches relative to the goal. She knows she doesn't have enough information to complete a Gaps Map. The next step is to put what information she does have into the Gaps Map format. Figure 3.6 shows what she has so far.

The Gaps Map has all the information that Jackie has gathered from her reframing interview and her two weeks of data gathering. She is still not ready to recommend solutions. She will meet with Leslie, Tom, and Kelly again to put the final pieces of the puzzle into the Gaps Map.

▶ 5. The Gaps Map Interview

Jackie hopes that one more meeting will help identify all the needed solutions. The new product mix is designed to gain a lift in sales, but that alone is not likely to solve the entire problem. It is becoming obvious that product knowledge training alone will not solve the entire problem either.

Jackie has a one-hour meeting scheduled with Leslie, Tom, and Kelly. She has to get a lot of critical information in that hour, so she needs to be organized to keep the meeting moving. She begins, not by sharing her Gaps Map, but by sharing and verifying the information she obtained from interviewing

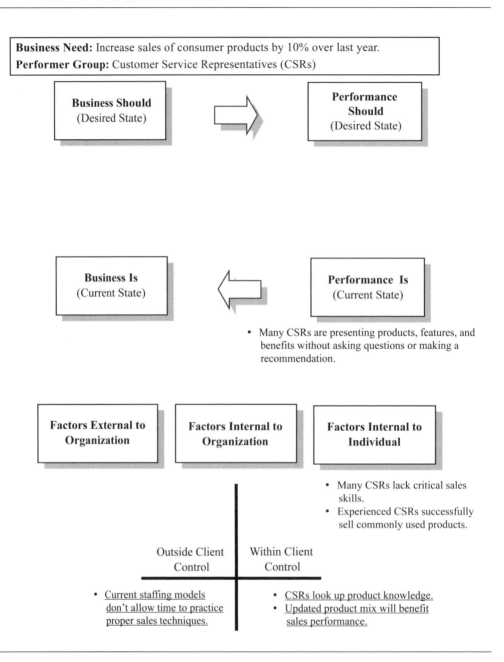

Business Need: Increase sales of consumer products by 10% over last year.
Performer Group: Customer Service Representatives (CSRs)

Business Should
(Desired State)

Performance Should
(Desired State)

Business Is
(Current State)

Performance Is
(Current State)

- Many CSRs are presenting products, features, and benefits without asking questions or making a recommendation.

Factors External to Organization

Factors Internal to Organization

Factors Internal to Individual

- Many CSRs lack critical sales skills.
- Experienced CSRs successfully sell commonly used products.

Outside Client Control

Within Client Control

- Current staffing models don't allow time to practice proper sales techniques.

- CSRs look up product knowledge.
- Updated product mix will benefit sales performance.

FIGURE 3.6   Gaps Map with Analysis Data

the three regional execs and the six branch managers. Leslie appeared surprised by the reports that many performers were not asking probing questions and making recommendations before referring to features and benefits. She was pleased to hear that the new product mix was favorably accepted by her managers. No one in the meeting was surprised to hear that the staffing models were hampering sales opportunities.

As the group began discussing the findings that Jackie presented, they began conjecturing about the possible meaning and solutions. In order to bring the conversation back to a strategic focus, Jackie asked Leslie to clarify, asking, "What *should* the desired business results be?" Leslie clarified the 10 percent increase in sales by stating that they needed to open ten thousand new accounts to generate revenue of $10,000,000. Jackie followed her response by asking, "What *is* the current business result?" Leslie answered that they were currently opening nine thousand accounts per year to generate revenue of $9,000,000. Jackie added this information to her map.

Jackie turned her attention to the entire group and asked, "Can you tell me what performance *is* getting us the current business results?" Everyone agreed that most of the customer service representatives (CSRs) were presenting products, features, and benefits without asking probing questions and making recommendations. This was supported by the interviews Jackie had with branch managers as well.

Jackie asked Leslie if she could tell her what the performance *should* be in order to achieve the desired business goal. Leslie was able to describe the sales behavior that she thought would bring about the best results. She described a questioning behavior and tying in product benefits, then making recommendations. Kelly, the training director, added that CSRs *should* rely on the available performance support tools as they go through the sales process.

Jackie was ready to move on to causes. She asked the group what might have *caused* the current poor business results. Tom pointed out that the recent merger activity had ramped up competition with more competitive prices. Leslie added that the new product mix she and her team were working on was also going to include better pricing to make them much more competitive.

Tom acknowledged that would help, but the staffing models were still going to make it difficult to practice proper sales techniques with that new product mix. He also pointed out that the long in-class training programs were further hampering the already stretched staffing models in the branches.

As the group began to get quiet again, Jackie asked if there was anything else they could think of that was *causing* the current business results. She heard that CSRs lacked sales skills, that they couldn't possibly memorize all the new product knowledge, and that the training was too long. She continued her questioning until she felt she got all she could from the group. Following that discussion, they moved on to discussing proposed solutions. At the conclusion of the meeting, they all agreed that Jackie and Kelly should talk to more branch managers and CSRs about the kind of training program they really needed. They agreed to meet again in one more week.

▶ 6. Completed Gaps Map with Solutions

Figure 3.7 shows the completed Gaps Map that Jackie used in her Friday meeting with Leslie, Tom, and Kelly. By the time the big meeting to present the recommended solutions arrived, Leslie had already convinced herself of the need for every potential solution proposed by the team.

- Kelly (Training) developed the new training programs, including performance support.

- Leslie (EVP) introduced the improved product mix and more competitive prices.

- Tom (HR) even persuaded most of the branches to augment their staffing during peak times.

- The redesigned training program using e-learning, classroom learning, and coaching would reduce time away from the branch.

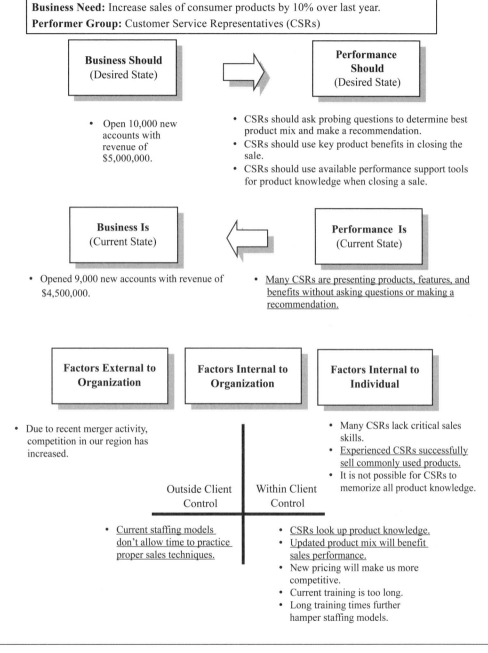

FIGURE 3.7   Completed Gaps Map with Solutions

■ In time, the behaviors of asking probing questions and making recommendations are expected to increase. They would ask managers to reinforce this behavior.

Jackie's only remaining task was to do some follow-up measurement and evaluation to assess the business impact and to determine the return on the investment in the combined solutions.

To watch a video role-play demonstration of a successful Gaps Map meeting, go to www.dhandshaw.com and click on the Resources tab.

THE NEXT PHASE . . .

The Needs/Gap Analysis phase helps you and your client identify key barriers to and enhancers of performance and the specific performance needed to achieve important business goals. Chapter 4 shows you how to use learning analysis to identify the exact performance and behaviors needed to deliver the desired business results.

Getting Real Value from Analysis

Chapter 3 showed you how to use the Gaps Map process to analyze business and performance needs. Now you're ready to work with the *Learning Analysis* phase of the Handshaw Instructional Design Model (see Figure 4.1). Included in this chapter are specific instructions on how and when to use four analysis steps, along with helpful tools and tips that guide their use. Keep in mind that you may not need to perform these analysis steps the same way every time you use the Analysis phase. One particularly useful concept covered in this chapter, called the *cost-vs.-risk rule,* is designed to help you determine how much time, if any, should be devoted to each analysis step. The analysis steps are as follows:

- Task analysis

- Audience analysis

- Learning culture analysis

- Delivery systems analysis

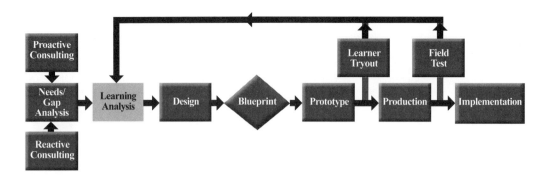

FIGURE 4.1   Handshaw Instructional Design Model: Learning Analysis

YOU CAN'T AFFORD *NOT* TO DO ANALYSIS

I've talked to a lot of trainers about analysis, and the most common reason most of them give for not doing analysis is "I don't have time." But here's what my experience has taught me—and I admit that it's counterintuitive. The *less* time I have to complete a project, the *more critical* it is to do analysis early. A friend and colleague, Damon Hearne, once succinctly characterized the importance of analysis with this statement: "If you don't have time to do analysis, be prepared to do design again and again and again." That's absolutely true. In fact, your best insurance policy against costly mistakes and missed deadlines is making the time to do the necessary amount of analysis. Here's a personal example to illustrate the point.

▶ An Expensive Lesson

A large bank in the Northeast wanted to use e-learning to demonstrate successful product sales skills to its financial consultants. It's important to mention that the product was new and a previous launch had gone so badly that the bank was in a hurry to take corrective action. That's why our request to complete a task analysis got so much pushback. The bank thought the best way to meet the deadline was to give its consultants the needed selling practice by using virtual role plays with interactive, prerecorded video clips.

The client just wanted our team to develop the video clip storyboards and the attendant e-learning program as quickly as possible. I explained that the purpose of the analysis was to document the process and write effective performance objectives. Our clients in the training department insisted that they would provide us with the performance objectives and that they would take on the job of explaining the process.

Soon the video clips were shot, and the scripted interactions were integrated into a powerful, interactive e-learning program. Our team designed a simulation that put the learners into an interactive conversation with their clients. Learners were able to select questions, and the video clips provided the appropriate client responses based on those choices. The training department clients were ecstatic and happily took credit for the wonderful design.

The business manager for the product line was not so pleased. "That's not how you're supposed to sell this product," the manager commented on first viewing the program. I knew we were in trouble. As it turned out, the performance objectives we followed were based on an outdated process and, of course, were completely wrong. We had to go back and rescript and reshoot the video clips. The e-learning program needed a great deal of revision to accommodate the new video clips and the updated sales process. Needless to say, we finished way behind schedule and way over budget. Expensive lessons are OK as long as you don't repeat them.

▶ Cost-vs.-Risk Rule

In this example, we ignored the cost-vs.-risk rule. This simple rule states: "As the project risk increases—whether that risk is cost, an aggressive schedule, and/or volatile content—so does the need for analysis." The corollary to the rule is: "Analysis is of little use without the appropriate stakeholders reviewing and signing off on the analysis data." In the preceding example, our team broke both of these rules:

- Because there was high risk due to a previously failed product rollout and the high production costs of interactive video role plays, we should have insisted on doing our own task analysis.

- The objectives given to us by the training client were reviewed by the appropriate subject matter experts but not by the stakeholder and managers.

Once we discovered the errors, we immediately conducted the appropriate level of task analysis. Based on a new and useful task analysis, all the performance objectives were rewritten. Based on the new performance objectives, the role-play scenarios and performance tests were rewritten. Based on the new scenarios, the new video clips were produced and new e-learning logic was written. You can see that my friend was right. We didn't do the necessary analysis, so we had to do our design again and again. It was a very expensive lesson.

TASK ANALYSIS THAT WORKS

Useful task analysis shows what a learner has to *know* and *do* in order to perform a specified task. Unfortunately, many designers develop task analyses that address just the observable, procedural steps a learner takes to complete a task. For a task analysis to represent all the processing that a learner must do to complete a task, the task analysis must show both knowledge and procedural behaviors. Ironically, designers who include only procedures in their task analyses tend to include mostly knowledge components in their instructional designs, which are based solely on content. More designers would make the time to develop task analyses if they could develop analyses that would save time and keep them out of trouble.

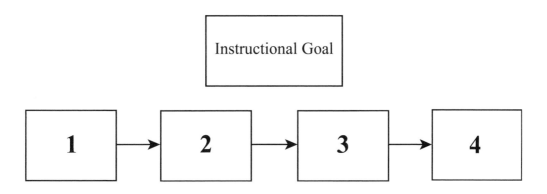

FIGURE 4.2   Procedural Task Analysis

▶ Four Types of Task Analysis

The four types of analysis—task, audience, learning culture, and delivery systems—are outlined in the text that follows. I firmly believe this methodology offers a real opportunity to derail the familiar "I don't have time" excuse for skipping analysis.

▶ Procedural Task Analysis

Procedural task analysis is easy to do. It documents the observable behaviors needed to complete a task. Robert Gagne categorized these easily observable behaviors as "procedural steps." Procedural steps are diagrammed from left to right, as shown in Figure 4.2. Instructional goals are accomplished when the learner is able to complete all the procedural steps in the correct order.

Your job as the designer is to observe and document the performer completing a task and then ask clarifying questions. That's it. Here are three important points to keep in mind when conducting procedural task analysis:

1. It includes procedural tasks and behaviors or skills.

2. It is diagrammed from left to right.

3. The task can be learned in any order but must be performed in the order shown on the task analysis.

▶ Hierarchical Task Analysis

A hierarchical task analysis is more difficult to develop than a procedural analysis because it requires that you document intellectual or knowledge-based tasks that are not directly observable. This means you have to ask questions to find out what a performer is "thinking" while completing a task. For example, you might have to ask: "How did you know which one of those [widgets, bolts, etc.] to pick?"; or: "How did you know which step to do next?"

There are two ways to develop a hierarchical task analysis (Figure 4.3). You can start with the instructional goal at the top of the analysis and work down to the simplest task at the bottom. Or you can start with the simplest task at the bottom of the hierarchy and work up to the instructional goal. Use whichever method works best for you.

In this hierarchical diagram, the learners must be able to master steps in a specific order. They must master steps 1, 2, and 3 before mastering step 4, and they must master step 5 before they can master step 6. When all the steps are completed or mastered in the right order, the instructional goal is achieved. Here are three points to remember when doing hierarchical task analysis:

1. It consists of knowledge or intellectual skills.

2. It is diagrammed from top to bottom or bottom to top, as you prefer.

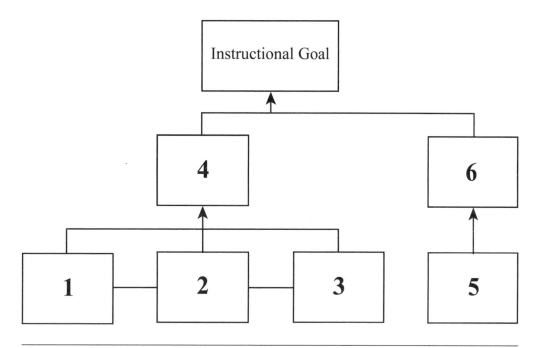

FIGURE 4.3 Hierarchical Task Analysis

3. The task must be learned and performed in the order shown on the task analysis.

▶ Combination Task Analysis

Combination task analysis (Figure 4.4) is exactly what you might assume. It combines the use of both procedural- and knowledge-based task analysis. Combination task analysis is an extremely useful type of task analysis since it allows for a more complete picture of what a performer has to *know* and *do* in order to complete a task.

This is the question you should ask yourself: "How can I possibly develop training that delivers results unless I know what a person has to know and do

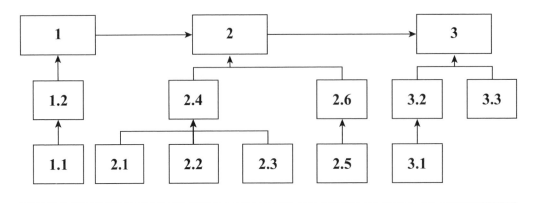

FIGURE 4.4   Combination Task Analysis

in order to complete the required task?" Trainers develop solutions every day without completing a task analysis. Most of them end up doing the design over again. Once you have learned this valuable skill, you will never approach another training project without using some form of task analysis.

▶ Cluster Task Analysis

Cluster task analysis (Figure 4.5) can be used when you come across content that must be categorized or processed so that content can be applied to perform a specific task. It is used most often when categorizing different levels of products or components, or even different types of compliance infractions.

▶ Assembling the Task Analysis Team

Developing a task analysis is difficult only when you try to do it by yourself. So it's best to assemble a team. First, you should find at least two subject matter experts. Assign one expert to actually perform the task while you and your other expert observe. The work goes faster and the final product is better since the outcome is based on different points of view. There may be some spirited debate, but this contributes to the usefulness of the final product.

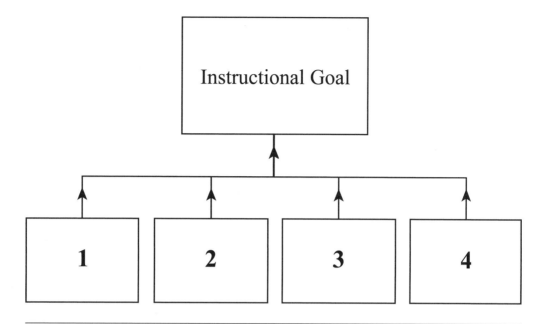

FIGURE 4.5 Cluster Task Analysis

If possible, you should observe the task completion in the actual environment—that is, out on the production line or other work environment. In the real world, that may not always be possible. So be creative. You might video the task and then perform the analysis while watching the video with your team. You might also meet with your experts via Internet-based collaborative tools.

Here is a typical list of stakeholders to consider including on your task analysis development team:

■ Managers or supervisors

■ Star performers

■ Subject matter experts (SMEs)

▶ Building a Combination Task Analysis

Developing a real task analysis takes time, so be prepared. Some consider it to be a tedious process; others find it entertaining and similar to solving a puzzle. Regardless of your first impression, the process gets easier and more rewarding with practice. In fact, you may find that the task analysis process results in more cooperation from your SMEs who understand—perhaps for the first time—what instructional designers do. Here are nine steps to help you create task analyses that save time and rework:

1. List all the tasks you can think of.

2. Determine which tasks are hierarchical or knowledge tasks and which ones are procedural tasks.

3. Complete your procedural task analysis by diagramming the main procedural tasks from left to right.

4. Diagram procedural subtasks from left to right.

5. Include additional procedural tasks not on your original list.

6. Complete your hierarchical task analysis by adding the appropriate knowledge tasks under your procedural tasks. You can start with the final task or with the entry-level tasks, whichever you find easier.

7. Look carefully for missing tasks or anything else in your analysis that doesn't make sense or seems out of place.

8. Walk through your analysis with a peer or colleague to ensure that your analysis makes sense.

9. Engage a different subject matter expert (not the one you used to do the original analysis) to evaluate your analysis for completeness and accuracy.

Figure 4.6 offers an example of a completed task analysis that should help you understand the process.

And here's a final "high-tech" tip. Nothing beats Post-it notes for task analysis. Start by putting one task on each Post-it note. Next, arrange your procedural steps from left to right, then complete the hierarchical steps. They are easy to change, rearrange, add to, or remove.

▶ Reviewing and Obtaining Sign-Off from Stakeholders

Your completed task analysis is a snapshot of the perfect performer following and completing the required task using the approved best practices. Don't assume that your analysis is ready for "prime time" until a review team has signed off on it. To decide who should be invited to participate in this task analysis review, I advise my clients to use the cost-vs.-risk rule. Weigh the cost or benefit of including too many or too few review team members. Having too many participants invites the possibility of disagreements among team members and risks time delays. Having too few participants brings a risk of missing key input from important stakeholders and subject matter experts, which would result in costly rework and project delays.

▶ Getting Good Feedback

The quality and usefulness of the feedback you receive depend on how well you prepare your reviewers. This means that you should explain task analysis and how it will be used. Once your reviewers understand task analysis data and how to interpret it, you can begin your questioning. Ask questions such as: "Is the analysis complete and accurate?" If the analysis is not complete, ask the reviewers to help you complete the missing steps. If the analysis is not

Sample Task Analysis – Recruiting – Determining Who to Contact

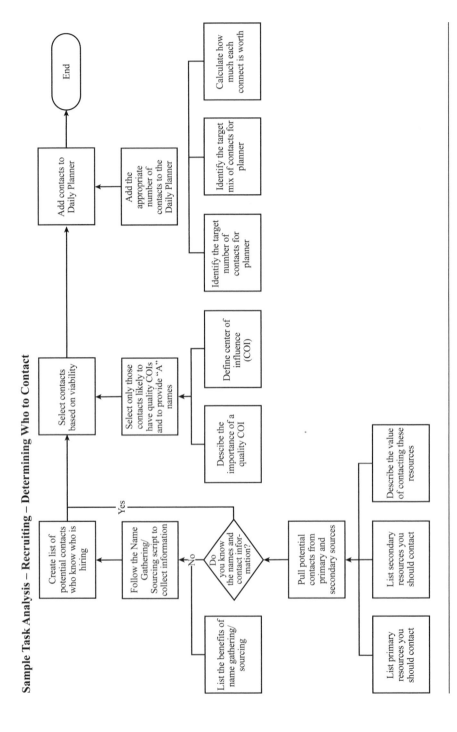

FIGURE 4.6   Combination Task Analysis Example

accurate, ask them to help you resolve the inaccuracies. If you get a response like "That's not how we do it," consider reframing your questions and asking for more useful feedback.

You'll likely get as many opinions about how the task should be performed as there are reviewers on the review team. Don't be discouraged. After all, this is why you asked for feedback on your task analysis in the first place. You want to verify the best practices before you begin developing training, not after.

AUDIENCE ANALYSIS FOR A REASON

Many instructional designers gather analysis data about their audience at the beginning of a project. In my experience, not all analysis data is always put to its best use. The bottom line on any analysis data is this: Analysis data is useful only if it has implications for how you will design training.

There are two categories of data to consider when conducting an audience analysis:

1. General characteristics, or demographics, of the intended audience

2. Entry behaviors, or data about what the learners already know about the required task

⮞ General Characteristics

When you walk into a classroom full of students, you can look around and you know immediately whom you will be talking with. You know how many are men and how many are women. You can even guess their approximate ages. This is important to you as you start a dialogue with your participants. You can use analogies, examples, and stories that you know are meaningful to them. You can begin to develop a personal relationship with your students.

This phenomenon is what learning psychologists call *social presence.* There is research that links social presence to successful learning. This is discussed in Chapter 8.

Gathering Data for General Characteristics

If your final product is e-learning or virtual classroom instruction for a large audience, you need to spend more time getting to know your audience before you make a lot of decisions about learning design. If you are designing instructor-led training for a small audience, you may not need to gather as much data. Use the cost-vs.-risk rule again.

The easiest method to obtain group demographic information about your audience is your human resources department. If you run into issues with confidentiality, assure your HR representative that all you need is general information about a group of performers. The following are examples of information that may prove useful to you:

- Gender mix, for example, 80 percent female, 20 percent male

- Average age and age range, for example, average age 58, age range from 35 to 66

- Racial mix, for example, 60 percent Hispanic, 20 percent Caucasian, 20 percent African-American

- Reading level, for example, 90 percent high school level, 10 percent literacy issues

- Years of experience, for example, average experience three years, experience range one to twelve years

If you're not able to get this information from the HR department, there are other ways of obtaining the data. There may be existing information in the form of marketing studies, customer support, or sales collateral where you can find information. If you have a high-visibility project with some high-risk factors, you can dig even deeper by conducting interviews with audience members, sending out surveys to audience members, or conducting interviews or surveys with a third party.

My company has developed training programs for more than sixty bank clients. You would think that after talking to tellers a few times, for instance, there would be nothing more to learn about them. Yet, every time we do interviews and observations in bank branches, we learn something new and critical for our learning design.

Implications for Learning Design

Analysis data really means nothing unless it has some implications for how you will design learning. The implications for general characteristics are often straightforward and even obvious. For instance, if you knew that 80 percent of your audience was female, you could use pictures, stories, and examples that contained women at least 80 percent of the time. But what if you didn't know this and your examples, pictures, names, and so forth, usually depicted men? This could be a significant distraction for your audience, and you could lose credibility. Fortunately, this kind of mistake is easily and inexpensively avoided.

As a matter of practice, audiences are often either homogeneous or heterogeneous. That is, they will be similar in gender, age, or education level (homogeneous), or they will not be similar at all (heterogeneous) and learning designs must cater to racial mix, gender, or a variety of ages or reading levels. In such cases, a quick survey of audience demographics helps you understand your audience and incorporate the results into your design. Figures 4.7 and 4.8 offer a good example of each audience type.

Reviewing and Revising General Characteristic Data

Before you rely on your audience analysis to make design decisions, make sure it's accurate. Send your results to the same review team that reviewed

GENERAL CHARACTERISTICS	IMPLICATIONS
Ratio—Female : Male = 88 : 12	• Most of the audience members are female. • Scenarios, examples, and graphics used in the training should reflect this statistic.

Length in current position:
  • Less than 1 year   83%
  • 1–5 years   17%
  • More than 5 years   0%
	• Most respondents are new to their jobs.
	• The training should focus on basic skills and new knowledge areas.
	• Learners should be offered a review of prerequisite skills.

Race:
  • 8% African American
  • 84% Caucasian
  • 8% Hispanic
	• Any examples of role plays, graphics, or pictures of participants or stories must depict mostly Caucasian participants with occasional African American and Hispanic participants.
	• Avoid any racial stereotypes or cultural references.

Reading Level:
  • 10%—12th grade and higher
  • 90%—10th grade to 12th grade
	• Use 10th grade as the target reading level.

FIGURE 4.7   Homogeneous Audience Analysis General Characteristics

your task analysis. You may want to send all of your analysis documents out at the same time to make it easier on your review team. Even if some members of your review team are not able to comment on the accuracy of your audience general characteristics, it will benefit them to see all the data you will use when you make design decisions. If they know what you know, they will be less likely to question your design decisions later, which means fewer changes and a more efficient work flow.

⮞ Entry Behaviors

By analyzing *entry behaviors,* which means analyzing what learners already know about what you are going to teach them, you may be able to individualize the instruction to fit your learners' needs (see Figure 4.9). It can be annoy-

GENERAL CHARACTERISTICS	IMPLICATIONS
Ratio—Female : Male = 54 : 46	• Audience members are equally divided between male and female. • Scenarios, examples, and graphics used in the training should reflect this statistic.

Length in current position:
  • Less than 5 years   23%
  • 5–10 years   23%
  • 10–20 years   48%
  • More than 20 years   6%
	• Most respondents are well established in their jobs and have additional industry experience in other roles or at other locations.
	• The training should focus on advanced skills and new knowledge areas, minimizing time spent on review of prerequisite skills.
	• If basic information must be included, learners should have the opportunity to opt out of those lessons.

Race:
  • 22% African American
  • 16% Asian
  • 34% Caucasian
  • 20% Hispanic
  • 8% Native American
	• Any examples of role plays, graphics, or pictures of participants or stories must depict a variety of races.
	• Avoid any racial stereotypes or cultural references.
	• Be inclusive in any way possible.

Reading Level:
  • 12%—12th grade and higher
  • 30%—10th grade to 12th grade
  • 42%—8th grade to 10th grade
  • 16%—below 8th grade
	• Use 8th grade as the target reading level.
	• Consider providing audio option for any students having difficulty reading text.

FIGURE 4.8 Heterogeneous Audience Analysis General Characteristics

ing for adult learners to be sent to training only to find that they already know some or all of what is being taught. Even if there are elements of the instruction that your learners might need, they will quickly become bored by having to review elements of the instruction that they already know. By the time they are introduced to something they don't know, they are already demotivated and inattentive.

If, for example, your solution calls for training on a new software system,

Entry Behaviors

Based on the work done during the audience analysis, the following assumptions can be made about the entry behaviors of the audience:

Assumption	Notes/Implications for Training
The system users are already familiar with the commercial lending process and work flow.	Training will assume that learners are already familiar with the overall commercial lending work flow and commercial loan products. Training should focus on tasks completed within the system and will not teach the concepts of the higher-level commercial lending process and phases.
	However, the training will teach system tasks within the context of the overall work flow so that learners understand how and when these tasks apply to the lending process.
	For example, one of the tasks included in the training will be entering a credit decision in the system. The content will assume that learners already know the concepts behind making the decision whether to approve the loan, so the task will focus on the logistics of navigating through the system to the appropriate tab and completing the required fields to enter the decision.
The system users already know how to complete commercial lending tasks in other systems.	Training will assume that learners are familiar with the steps for completing tasks in other systems, such as MDM and Moody's. Training should focus only on tasks completed within the system and should not teach tasks completed in other systems.
	When a system task requires work to be done outside of the system, the training will describe that there is a need for additional work to be done outside of the system, and that the learner (or other role) would complete this work. Training will then describe how the data returns to the system and continue with describing the next step as a result of that input. It will not cover the steps taken to complete tasks in other systems.
	For example, the training will cover the task to spread the financials. It may say something along the lines of, "You would now go to Moody's and spread the financials. Once you have finished, the data will be communicated to the system. You will now have a task in your Work Center to review the spreading information on the Financials tab. To do so . . ."
One of the goals for implementing the system is to build and enforce a consistent commercial lending process across all locations.	With the new system, we are working toward a standard global process across all locations for commercial lending. Training will reflect the standard work flow, and will not address specific differences in work flow among affiliates.
	Training should acknowledge this approach early in the curriculum by communicating that the training covers the overall commercial lending process and that there may be some specific differences based on the individual learner's branch.

FIGURE 4.9   Audience Analysis Entry Behaviors Example

the entry behaviors become obvious. Everyone needs to learn everything. If the required training also addresses how to use the system to do a particular job—and it probably should—you will need more information on entry behaviors.

If you are developing e-learning, you may need to design the course to adapt to learners with different entry behaviors. One of the great benefits of e-learning is that it can be individualized. But you can take advantage of this benefit only if you are aware of the different needs of different learners.

Gathering Data for Entry Behaviors

Gathering data for entry behaviors is not quite as easy as asking HR for audience demographic data, but it can be done efficiently if you gather the data during the task analysis process. Simply ask about different learners' capabilities in completing each task as you complete the hierarchical portion of your analysis. Figure 4.10 is an example of an entry behavior in a hierarchical task analysis.

Implications for Learning Design

In general, the implications for your design are that you'll need to customize instruction to fit the different learner needs. For example, you can map different job tasks and only prescribe module completion based on the job each learner performs. This is especially effective when using learning objects with e-learning.

You can also include a pretest to measure what your learners know and then prescribe instructional modules for those not achieving mastery on the pretest. You might allow your learners to self-select the modules they need without any other screening or pretest.

Reviewing and Revising Entry Behavior Data

The review of your entry behavior data is usually more critical and time consuming than the review of your general characteristics data. You only need to identify trends for general characteristics, but you need detailed data that

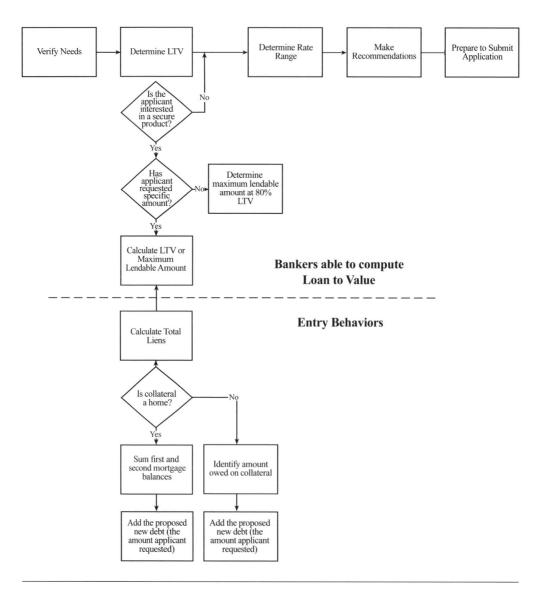

FIGURE 4.10   Task Analyses with Entry Behaviors

follows along with your task analysis for entry behaviors. The subject matter experts who worked with you to create the task analysis should understand the entry behavior decisions, since they helped you create the task analysis. Be sure you provide an explanation of how the entry behaviors work with the task analysis.

This small investment of time yields a big payoff in the cases where you really do need to accommodate different audiences with different needs.

THE LEARNING CULTURE—YOUR BIGGEST OPPORTUNITY

Leveraging culture in learning design and implementation was the biggest opportunity I never knew I had until a client taught me a valuable lesson about culture. We were developing a manager training program for a large company. My client, a senior vice president of human resources, told me she wanted the new managers to "find themselves in the company story within one week of beginning his or her new job."

At the time, I didn't really know what she meant by "finding themselves in the company story," but I do now! Her company made and sold doughnuts in a chain of retail stores nationwide. Managing a doughnut shop seemed straightforward enough. At the request of our client, we began to learn about their culture. The company knew it was not just in the doughnut business; it was really in the customer experience business. We learned how their chain of doughnut stores worked to create what they called "magic moments" for their customers. "Magic moments" were created every time a customer walked into one of their stores and smelled fresh coffee brewing and doughnuts frying. These "moments" were created as customers watched fresh doughnuts being made from behind a glass wall and observed the doughnuts getting their sugar glaze on a conveyor belt. And, of course, these lasting memories were created through great customer service. Simply teaching managers how to make doughnuts, keep the store clean, and manage finances was not enough. Our challenge was this: How do we teach their store managers the basics of running a doughnut shop while instilling in them the importance of "making magic moments" and creating a memorable customer experience?

We leveraged the company's strong corporate culture in each module of the store managers' training program. Instead of calling it "Store Managers' Training Program," we renamed it "Making Magic Moments." Each new module began with a story from a customer about an aspect of the experience that he or she felt was special. The company received hundreds of stories each year from customers, so we had lots to choose from. We related a particular story to some element of the upcoming module and then continued to refer to the story and the importance of that story to the module topic. Our learners "found themselves in the company's story," and our client was delighted. We also learned a valuable lesson about leveraging culture to support learning.

▶ Gathering Data for the Learning Culture

Gathering data for learning culture analysis can be time consuming. But the good news for internal practitioners is that you'll need to do this just once and then update your data from time to time. External consultants should consider this step as a necessary task that is often critical to your client's success. Clients often reuse the data you collect in their own learning designs.

The best way to accurately gauge the pulse of corporate culture is to talk to employees of the company and conduct in-person interviews when possible. Phone interviews with sample learners, managers, and stakeholders are also quite effective. These interviews are usually conducted with a prepared list of questions, but interviewers often pursue different lines of questioning based on responses.

Once you have completed enough interviews, a report is produced that defines the current learning and/or corporate culture. Most new corporate initiatives involve some kind of change that can be enhanced or challenged by existing culture. For example, if the organization wanted to introduce a new m-learning initiative, you would need to know more about the following issues:

- How do employees receive learning?

- How is learning measured?

- Are learners held accountable for their training and performance?

- Is technical support for the learning delivery system well received?

When a learning solution is designed to accompany some type of important corporate initiative, a corporate and/or learning culture analysis is absolutely necessary to make sure your client achieves the business results that the change initiative was designed to produce. Culture can be your best friend or your worst enemy when it comes to introducing change.

Culture can work to your advantage if some formal change management work is being done to support a major corporate change initiative. If so, you should coordinate learning culture findings with this change management plan. Your research will answer some of these questions:

- How are learners held accountable for using the training and performance?

- How well do the immediate supervisor and manager support the learning effort and achievement of the task?

- What's the link between learning and performance improvement?

- How do the learning and business goals align?

➤ Procedures and Implications for Learning Design

You may not always find ways to enhance your learning design from your learning culture analysis data. But even if you don't leverage this data in the course design, you will almost always use the data in your implementation plan, since culture often creates barriers to new corporate and learning initiatives.

After you've gathered data from employees, managers, and business stakeholders, take the following steps to define and use culture to your advantage. My client from the doughnut company example taught me that "every organization has a culture, whether it is intentional or not."

Here's how you can make your culture intentional and leverage it to help you deliver business results. The learning culture analysis is designed to help the organization:

- **Define the business need for the initiative:** Step 1 in leveraging your culture in learning design and implementation is to define the business need for the initiative. If you have completed the performance consulting phase, you have already defined the business goal.

- **Articulate the vision and inspire champions:** Once you identify the business goal, you need to find someone in the organization to help you turn that goal into a vision. The vision, in turn, will be used to inspire people to follow and support the goal. Every change initiative has early adopters who are beneficial in helping to bring about change. You need to find these early adopters and make them champions of your new initiative. That's why developing relationships is so important.

- **Identify internal and external partners:** The more internal partners you have on your side, the greater your chance for success. You need line managers, subject matter experts, and even some of the star performers on your side. Recruit them to your project team for brainstorming, reviews, and even early testing of prototype lessons. This is how you leverage culture to support a sustainable change. You and your client may also need to identify external partners for dedicated work on technology or marketing efforts that may be missing from your internal partner list.

- **Connect the learner with the desired culture:** This is a critical step directly tied to the design of your instructional events and implementation plan. There are many creative ways to use what you learned about culture to enhance your instructional design and make the learning sustainable, but it's only through learning about culture that you'll be able to make these connections.

- **Align the initiative with the organization's brand, values, and business objectives:** In the aforementioned doughnut company example, the company had a strong corporate culture. We found some gaps in the existing learning culture and made creative use of an interesting technique to leverage the corporate culture to make a lasting impression for learners in the manager training course.

- **Help learners find themselves in the organization's story:** Our design in the doughnut company example was repeated over and over with each new module of instruction. Clearly, the design we developed helped our new learners quickly find their role in the organization's story.

- **Identify methods to measure success:** In Chapter 5 you will discover new methods for measuring the success of sustainable culture change and how well the initiative supports the achievement of the organization's business goals.

Adapted from Barbara Thornton, People Development.

➧ Reviewing and Revising Learning Culture Data

Learning culture analysis review requires some finesse to deal with subjective reviewer comments or defensive reactions to collected data. Focus first on whether or not the data is complete and accurate, and always be objective in how you present the content in your report. Your objectivity increases the odds that reviewers will also be objective in their reviews.

As with all analysis reviews, including more people on the review team may require more discussion, but it is far better to resolve differences before you make design decisions. It also serves the purpose of keeping everyone who has an interest in the project informed about what is going on. The review process also helps prevent the negative effects of "swoopers." Swoopers are people who say nothing until the end of the project and then swoop in and want to make major changes. Sound familiar?

You can mitigate the swooper impact by including a sign-off letter with your review documents. Make sure you agree ahead of time with your review team on a reasonable time for them to review and sign off on the documents. Ask them to return the sign-off letter with their comments by a deadline date, and stress that comments received after the deadline will not be considered. This action doesn't ensure that you will never have last-minute changes, but it is a very helpful tool to at least reduce the occurrence of these disruptive changes.

DELIVERY SYSTEMS ANALYSIS

Instructional designers readily accept blended solutions and the idea that different parts of their instructional design might be delivered by a variety of media and delivery systems including virtual classroom, e-learning, and m-learning, in addition to instructor-led training. However, one challenge of blended solutions is matching the design to the appropriate delivery method and media. Analysis can help you with this challenge.

◗ Gathering Data for Delivery Systems Analysis

If you're an internal designer, taking a survey of all the delivery systems in use in your organization shouldn't take long, and you may even discover a few new delivery systems or techniques in the process (see Figure 4.11). As you compile your list, keep track of the positive and negative traits of each delivery system. If use data exists, include information on how each different delivery system was received by its intended audience. You should be able to gather all this information from colleagues in your training group. Note that, as an internal practitioner, you have the option of revising this document on a regular basis. If you are an external practitioner, it is absolutely necessary to complete a delivery systems analysis before you begin making design decisions. It can be embarrassing to discover that the technology you selected does not exist at your client's facility.

◗ Implications for Learning Design

It's not uncommon for clients to ask a designer to develop an e-learning program or a two-day workshop based on previous success. As you learned in Chapter 2, the best strategy is to nod your head, listen attentively, and then go do your homework in preparation for a reframing meeting. You'll find your delivery systems analysis a useful decision-making resource, especially when you use it as supportive data to match each performance objective to the most appropriate delivery system or media option. Chapter 5 offers an opportunity to work through a structured process for making media and delivery system choices.

◗ Reviewing and Revising Delivery Systems Analysis Data

The delivery system analysis review process offers the opportunity to discover a variety of opinions on which delivery systems work well and which ones don't. Keep in mind that the differing opinions of your review team repre-

The following sections outline the target delivery platform(s). Note that, as much as possible, our program materials should operate within the same requirements as the system itself.

Specification	Data	Notes
Operating Systems:	• Windows XP SP3 or newer	
Browsers:	• IE 8 is specified as enterprise standard	
Plug-ins Available:	• Flash Player version 9 (or newer) • Adobe Reader 9.0 and above • Java versions 1.5-1.6	
Screen Resolution:	• 1024×768	Due to the size of the system application screens, the larger the available space the better. Previous content for this system was developed at a browser-safe 1024×768 resolution. At that size, screens required scrolling in both directions.
Sound:	• Sound cards and speakers are listed as "optional" in current Online Content Standards.	If the use of sound is desired, further investigation is recommended.
Learner Tracking:	• Course hosting and learner tracking will be through the LMS—vendor hosted. • AICC communication is preferred, but SCORM 1.2 is also accepted.	Will need to discuss level of completion tracking during the Design phase. SCORM 1.2 is not preferred due to cross-domain browser security issues—but this is potentially mitigated by hosting course content on vendor's servers.
Connectivity:	• Broadband or better	File size has been noted as being of some concern in a small number of branches. Video, audio, and other potentially large file types should be used with some caution.

Current Courseware:	• Estimated 900 hours of courseware is deployed through LMS.
	• 90% custom, 10% off-the-shelf
	• Courseware developed internally using the following tools:
	  ○ Articulate (Primary)
	  ○ Camtasia
	  ○ Captivate
	  ○ Flash
	  ○ Recorded WebEx/LiveMeeting sessions
		Previous system content was developed using Captivate version 5. Since Captivate is used internally, any existing development standards should be considered during the Design phase.
		
		Some guidance is available for courseware publishing standards for each of the listed tools in the Online Content Standards document.
		
		Current courseware is well received, but is too long and requires more opportunity for practice. Feedback is to spend less time explaining, more time doing.

FIGURE 4.11 Delivery Systems Analysis Example

sent the data that you'll use in the next phase of the project to make a final decision. If you collect data that you think is irrelevant or inaccurate, you can always disregard it or investigate it further later on. Analysis data is objective. It's just data. Finally, ask your review team to evaluate the delivery systems analysis report for completeness and accuracy and make any revisions before you move on.

THE NEXT PHASE . . .

The purpose of investing time in the Analysis phase is to save time during the rest of your project. Analysis is not a decision-making phase; it is a data collection phase. In the Design phase, you will have to make many design decisions. Rather than making decisions based on opinions or preferences, you can make good design decisions based on data. The information you gather during the Analysis phase will serve you as you progress through the rest of the instructional design process and will help keep you focused on business results.

CHAPTER 5

Connecting Objectives to Measurement

Based on the current trend to do more with less, many instructional designers feel pressured to skip analysis all together, or at least take shortcuts when it comes to conducting analysis. As you learned in Chapter 4, I encourage designers to take a flexible approach to analysis and consider how much analysis will yield a positive business or performance impact. If you have applied the cost-vs.-risk rule to analysis, you will have the right amount of data to help you make good decisions in the Design phase of the model (see Figure 5.1).

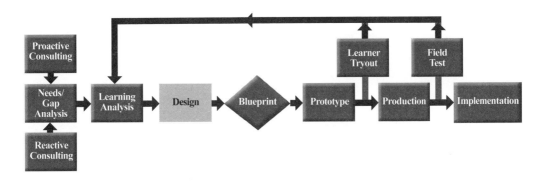

FIGURE 5.1   Handshaw Instructional Design Model: Design

THE REAL PURPOSE OF PERFORMANCE OBJECTIVES

Regardless of whether they write objectives, many instructional designers don't take advantage of all the things performance objectives can do for them.

If you think you are *not* getting the most out of your performance objectives, here are three good uses for them:

1. **An advanced organizer for learners:** Objectives give learners an advanced organizer, or a cue for what's coming up in the course. In conducting our own research about the use of objectives as an advanced organizer, we tracked several hundred users of an online course to determine whether they read the first page of a course containing objectives or skipped the page. Only 10 percent of learners chose to view the page with the objectives, which means that 90 percent made no attempt to view the learning objectives for the course. Based on interviews with learners in the 10 percent group, we found they always chose to read objectives before beginning a lesson. Despite the fact that many learners don't use objectives as an advanced organizer, we concluded that you should make them available.

2. **A contract for the entire design team to describe required outcomes:** Think of the Franklin Covey concept of starting with the end in mind. Objectives provide an up-front understanding of project outcomes among the client, the project sponsor, and the lead instructional designer. In addition, objectives are highly effective tools for managing team member expectations. Objectives offer a concise and definitive description of required learner behavior that will be expected upon successful completion of the instruction. Well-written objectives also help instructional designers understand the required level of learned

capability and provide facilitators with key insight into learner requirements.

3. **A tool for designing measurement strategies:** The most powerful and useful application of performance objectives is in formulating a successful measurement strategy. To achieve this outcome, you must use Gagne's five-part format for writing objectives. The key to this format is in the *action* portion of the objective, which describes how to perform the required task. Our standard practice is to write one objective for each main task in the task analysis. Writing the action portion is easy because we use the subtasks from the task analysis to describe exactly what steps a learner takes to perform the task. Following this path provides a detailed and accurate description of how the task should be performed. Once you know how the task should be measured, it becomes obvious how the task should be taught. This in turn helps you define your instructional strategy and media selection without having to guess what might work.

HOW TO WRITE USEFUL PERFORMANCE OBJECTIVES

Writing performance objectives is an effective use of your time, whether or not learners use them. This section provides proven ways to write objectives that help you make better design decisions.

There are several reasons why I favor using Gagne's five-part format for writing objectives. The five parts are:

1. **Situation:** The stimulus for performing the task.

2. **Learned Capability:** The verb that describes the level of capability being learned.

3. **Object:** The object, or the "what," of the capability verb.

4. **Action:** Description of "how" the learner will perform the task.

5. **Tools/Constraints:** Description of specific tools or methods that must be used to perform the task and any constraints such as time or mastery level. This may be considered an optional part if tools and constraints don't apply to the task in question.

▶ Performance Objective Example

We always write performance objectives exactly as shown in the following example because it's easier for our clients to read and understand the results of the task analysis. For example, if the main task from your analysis is to "recommend the best product mix," then the five parts of the objective might be as follows:

1. **Situation:** Given a prospective customer

2. **Learned Capability:** the learner will be able to recommend

3. **Object:** the best product mix

4. **Action:** by asking probing questions, presenting related benefits, and handling objections

5. **Tools/Constraints:** in every sales transaction.

We write our performance objectives exactly as shown in this example. This format makes it easier for us to write objectives, and it makes it easier for our clients to read and understand them. One thing you have to know is where to get the information. We always do a task analysis, and that is what makes writing performance objectives easy. Here is how it's done:

1. The **situation** comes from whatever event prompts the learner to have to perform the task, which in this case is the existence of a prospective customer.

2. The **capability verb** and the object come directly from the main tasks in the task analysis, which in this case is "Recommend the best product mix."

3. The **action** portion comes from the subtasks subsidiary to the main task. The subtasks are: ask probing questions, present related benefits, and handle objections. Note that each subtask also contains a verb and an object.

4. The relevant **constraint** in this case is that the task must be performed as described "in every sales transaction."

The most common mistake made in the process of writing performance objectives is trying to complete them without first conducting a full task analysis. While you might be able to identify important elements without first analyzing the task, it is also likely that you'll overlook an important element or make other critical mistakes. More important, if you write performance objectives without doing a task analysis, you'll run a substantial risk that a learning design won't be linked to either your client's business or job performance needs.

⮞ Levels of Learned Capability

Another common mistake in writing performance objectives is in the use of capability verbs. For instance, the verb *understand* is commonly used in performance objectives. But it is difficult to measure the level of understanding or specify what level of understanding is required to perform a task successfully on the strength of the verb *understand*. Good performance objectives are both observable and measurable.

Fortunately, some effective taxonomy tools are available to help nail down meaning and increase understanding so that designers can accurately identify expected learner outcomes. Benjamin Bloom's classic learning objective taxonomy is one well-known methodology. Gagne's Five Levels of Learned Capability is another. You can search the Internet for these two topics if you are not familiar with them. Regardless of the method you use, your objectives must convey clear learning outcomes for learners, team members, facilitators, and other stakeholders. You'll also find that using the appropriate verbs to describe the correct level of learned capability is critical to getting real value out of performance objectives.

➡ Getting Real Value from Your Performance Objectives

If you practice writing objectives in this five-part format for a while, it becomes a relatively easy and efficient process—that is, if you start with a task analysis. Now that you have performance objectives, let's make sure you get the most benefit from them.

Your learners probably can't use your five-part objectives in their current format. When you use the five-part format, your objectives will be too long and cumbersome for your learners to easily understand. The objectives may need a little editing to make them learner friendly.

While a task analysis is useful for many subject matter experts, it may not work for stakeholders. The performance objective is another way to present the information contained in a task analysis. People may not always respond well to your task analysis, especially if they don't like flowcharts, but they will usually be able to understand and relate to your performance objectives. These five-part objectives are your best shot at getting everyone on your design team to agree on exactly what the learner outcomes should be.

I often hear designers complain about scope creep and that clients keep changing their minds about what the learning should contain and how things should be done. When I ask them if they use performance objectives tied to a task analysis, they usually say, "No, I don't have time for that."

▶ Using the Action Portion to Design Tests

The action portion of the objective practically designs your tests for you. Consider the following example.

> **Main task: Write a five-part performance objective.**
>
> 1. **Situation:** Given a list of incomplete objectives
>
> 2. **Learned Capability:** the learner will demonstrate
>
> 3. **Object:** the rules for writing five-part objectives
>
> 4. **Action:** by rewriting each objective
>
> 5. **Tool/Constraint:** in a five-part format.

By looking at the action portion, which explains how the learner should perform the task, it becomes obvious how to measure mastery of that task. Neither a multiple-choice question nor a true/false question will do in this case. To measure this objective, you must give the learner a list of main tasks from a task analysis and evaluate how well the learner can actually write them into a five-part format. This example is an actual objective from my workshop on how to write performance objectives.

Here is another example.

Main task: Perform equipment check.

1. **Situation:** Before entering the water

2. **Learned Capability:** the learner will demonstrate the procedure

3. **Object:** for checking his/her buddy's dive gear

4. **Action:** by testing the bladder inflate button, testing the bladder air release button, checking all buckles and fasteners, checking the regulator for airflow, checking the safe second regulator for airflow, and checking for proper weights

5. **Tools/Constraints:** with 100 percent accuracy.

You don't really have to know anything about scuba diving to know how to measure this important performance objective. We have a saying in the dive shop where I used to teach scuba: "It's only life support"—hence, the constraint requiring 100 percent accuracy. Obviously, I had to observe the person performing this equipment check and grade the results using a checklist. It is easy to design a test for this objective, even if you know nothing about diving. You would observe an expert performing this equipment check, write down all the steps you observed as subtasks under the main task of performing an equipment check, and then use the task analysis to write the objective. Since the capability verb says that the learner has to demonstrate something, you know you have to use a performance test. You would observe the learner testing his or her buddy's dive gear and make sure the learner included all the steps listed in the action portion.

THE *WAY* YOU MEASURE CHANGES EVERYTHING

Measurement is one of the most misunderstood aspects of instructional design. Learners and clients have a natural tendency to resist being held accountable to a standard. That's a problem, since your business partner status requires that you measure your success in order to demonstrate the real business results it achieves.

Maybe your client only needs to verify that training was provided. Measurement could be your opportunity to show whether or not people are achieving results. This can be your opportunity to be a performance partner and add real value again, instead of being just an order taker.

Measurement is not just making up a few multiple-choice questions and developing a test. You must predict whether a learner can actually apply mastery of the performance objectives and then achieve the required business results. This is called *predictive validity*. The term *validity* describes whether a test measures the content or objectives that the test is intended to measure. *Predictive validity* describes whether the outcome of the test will predict the performance of the learner on the job. Obviously, your tests are of little value if they can't predict future performance.

Fortunately, there are only two mistakes you can make in developing tests. First, you must select the right type of testing instrument. Once you have selected the right type of testing instrument, you need to write your test questions correctly. The way you measure is determined mostly by the type of testing instrument you select, and that is determined by your performance objective.

Look at the following example of a five-part objective and see if you can determine the best way to measure whether your learners could actually perform this task on the job. Now you can see why I prefer the five-part format. It's the verb describing the *level of learned capability* and the *action* portion that really tell you how to measure the objective. As you can see in this example, not everything can be measured by using a multiple-choice question. This example would require a performance test.

Main task: Handle special ATM items.

1. **Situation:** Given ATM deposits

2. **Learned Capability:** the learner will handle

3. **Object:** special ATM items

4. **Action:** by processing unreadable envelopes, processing empty envelopes, processing nonnegotiable envelopes, and processing foreign items

5. **Tools/Constraints:** with 100 percent accuracy.

▶ Measurement Strategy

The way you measure can be determined easily and consistently with the use of a well-written performance objective. If the verbs you select really do a good job of describing the required level of learned capability, you will find it much easier to select testing instruments that can predict future performance on the job and deliver results.

Another thing to think about when selecting your testing instrument is practicality. There may be an ideal way to measure, and there may be a practical way to measure. As you begin to use your well-written performance objectives to select testing instruments, you will find that more and more objectives require some sort of performance test, which may be time consuming and expensive to conduct. The next section will help you make the best compromise on test selection.

USING OBJECTIVES TO DESIGN MEASUREMENT STRATEGY

In order to design your measurement strategy, you need to know what types of testing instruments are available. In the corporate world, only criterion-referenced tests (CRTs) are acceptable. Many of the tests you took in school were norm-referenced tests. You were measured against the norm, or the test scores of other students. A good test score didn't necessarily mean you had mastered all the objectives; it just meant you did better than your peers.

The criteria in CRTs are the performance objectives. You can see why it is important to measure to the performance objectives rather than to the norm. We do a lot of work in the nuclear industry. Our clients want to know that their learners can master the performance objectives at 90 percent or even 100 percent. It's not acceptable for them to just be better than the next person.

There are two categories of CRTs:

1. Objective tests

2. Performance tests

▶ Objective Tests

Objective tests are relatively easy to develop and easy to score. They work well when used properly and in the right setting. The most commonly used types of objective test questions include:

- True/false

- Matching and ranking

- Completion or fill-in-the-blank

■   Single select (commonly called multiple choice) and multiple
select

Objective questions work well with e-learning. The selection of questions
for e-learning is partly responsible for the confusion about the appropriate
use of different question types. A lot of test question selection happens this
way: "Let's see, I've written four multiple-choice questions in a row; maybe I
should throw in a true/false question next."

When you developed your task analysis, you picked good action verbs for
your learned capability. Then you used those good verbs to make sure you
described the required level of learned capability in your performance objective. Now use that verb to help pick the appropriate type of testing instrument. If the verb you've used is *select,* or something similar, you can use a
single-select question because you are selecting something from a list. If the
verb is *know* or *recall,* you can use a completion question because you have to
recall the correct word or words.

Now you can see why it is so important for you to visualize and describe
the exact level of learned capability that is required for successful completion
of a task. If you have measured a learner for his or her ability to select an
answer from a list using a single-select question, and the job or task requires
the learner to problem-solve, which should be done with a performance test,
your measurement will not have the level of predictive validity that your client needs. Invalid test results may lead you to think your learners will achieve
the required performance, when in real practice they may not. If you can't
predict performance, you can't achieve business results.

▶ Performance Tests

A performance test is exactly what it sounds like. A learner must actually
perform some kind of task, be observed by an expert, and be scored on
how successfully the task is completed. These tests may be time consuming
and difficult to complete. For example, if the task requires an engineer to

inspect and service a pump in a nuclear plant, the high risk of poor performance justifies the time and expense. Sometimes performing a simulation of the task, or performing the task with a scored computer simulation, suffices. You have to be able to apply the cost-vs.-risk rule in each new situation.

Performance tests can take a variety of forms; their application is limited only by your imagination and creativity. Formulating a performance test begins with a review of the performance objective. Pay close attention to the learned capability verbs and the action portion used in the objective. These sections are solid clues to creating appropriately structured performance tests. For example, in a sales or interviewing/counseling situation, using a role play is a very effective performance test strategy. Real or virtual simulations work well for tasks that involve setting up or using and/or maintaining equipment.

The following example shows the steps from task analysis to creating the performance objective and then selecting a type of testing instrument (or measurement strategy).

Main task: Escalate a question or concern.

1. **Situation:** Given a question or concern while performing tasks

2. **Learned Capability:** the learner will escalate

3. **Object:** a question or concern to a manager

4. **Action:** by logging the issue and notifying the appropriate manager.

   Measurement Strategy: Record actions taken during a branch simulation/role play.

You design your measurement strategy at this part of the instructional design process because you will use it to determine your instructional strategy. You present both of these strategies to your project team in the blueprint meeting before you proceed to develop a prototype. You don't actually have to write or construct your tests at this point, although you could. In this chapter on design, you have solved the big problem of selecting the appropriate testing instrument. When you get to Chapter 9, in the Production phase, you will learn how to solve the other problem with test development: how to write better test questions.

Another aspect of testing that you should deal with at this point in your design process is the role of feedback in your testing. Some schools of thought say that measurement of learner mastery should not include feedback. The purpose of final mastery tests is just to measure. I am so convinced of the role of feedback in the learning process that I prefer never to miss an opportunity to provide feedback. This decision can be determined by your learning culture or by the confines of time and practicality.

To make it easier for you to begin selecting appropriate testing instruments, you can refer to the following performance support tool. As you can see, it depends heavily on the learned capability verb from your performance objective. This is exactly how you use your performance objectives to design your measurement strategy. (See Figure 5.2.)

▶ Scoring Tests

Scoring objective test items is relatively easy once you determine what constitutes a passing score. I always encourage clients to set 90 percent as a passing score in most industries, but for high-risk environments such as the nuclear energy and healthcare industries, clearly 100 percent mastery is an absolute requirement. Of course, a particular organization's culture and attitude about accountability can have a significant impact in determining a passing score.

Types of Test Items

Behavior from Objective	Fill in the blank	Multiple Choice	Matching	True/False	Performance	Essay	Oral
State	X						X
Identify		X					X
Classify	X	X	X			X	X
Discuss	X					X	X
Define	X					X	X
Select		X	X	X			
Discriminate		X	X	X			
Solve	X	X		X	X	X	X
Develop	X	X			X	X	
Locate		X	X	X	X	X	X
Construct					X	X	X
Generate	X				X	X	
Choose		X			X		
Originate					X	X	X
Execute					X	X	
Demonstrate	X				X	X	X

FIGURE 5.2 Selecting Test Types for Objectives (adapted from John A. Gretes)

Scoring performance tests is more challenging because achieving objective measurement is difficult. So, to measure *how* someone should perform a task, simply refer to the action portion of the objective or review the subtasks from the task analysis.

Note that consistent measurement and consistent business results for your client are hardwired together. That's why using an objective checklist process for measuring performance tests allows for the objective measurement of even "soft skills," which is so important to your client.

To be truly useful to you and your client, tests must be valid and reliable. A *valid* test is one that measures the objectives or content it is intended to measure. The *reliability* of a test indicates how consistently your tests measure results against those of a large number of learners. Simply put, if the tests in your design fulfill both these criteria, then your client can consider the results to be valuable business information.

▶ The Impact of Culture on Measurement Strategy

Organizational culture directly influences your ability to measure the impact of the learning activities you design. Some organizations are less supportive of measurement than others for a variety of reasons, such as philosophical resistance or financial constraints. Clearly, you need the backing of the client organization to achieve any real business results.

A lot of companies identify tests as *assessments* or use other terms to avoid the word *test*. To me, the word *assessment* means "appraisal." The meanings and usages of the words *measurement* and *evaluation* also vary among different organizations. *Measurement* means that you determine the extent to which something happens. *Evaluation* is also a good word, with a different meaning from that of *measurement*. *Evaluation* means that you fix a value to something or determine the worth of something. Language is an important expression of culture, so pay attention to the language used in learning culture interviews.

USING MEASUREMENT TO DESIGN INSTRUCTIONAL STRATEGY

You may notice when your clients approach you for a training request—one that seems perfect for reframing—that they offer an instructional strategy for you to implement for them. They are asking you to participate with them in *solution jumping.* When someone shares a performance problem or a training need with you, you probably find it easy to jump to a strategy for instruction. You may have done something to address a similar situation in the past or perhaps the obvious solution just comes to you. Sometimes, your client's idea or your first intuitive idea for an instructional strategy is just what you need. In other cases, your intuitive solution may cause you to overlook better possibilities. Sometimes, making instructional strategy decisions not based on data can be a big mistake.

You have learned so far that in order to measure the capabilities of your learners in a useful way, you must have well-written performance objectives. You have also learned how necessary it is to know in a detailed way what learners must be able to do to achieve business results, so you created a task analysis to verify the required performance. Now that you have a measurement strategy based on your work, you can use it to formulate an instructional strategy. Once you know how to measure your learners, it becomes much easier to determine the best way to provide instruction.

▶ Instructional Strategy

The real world and perfect processes are often at odds. In the real world, a client may approach you with a training request and then offer an instructional strategy. If you've done similar training recently, you might be able to articulate an obvious solution, or perhaps you decide the client's solution is good on its own. Following this path may or may not be a mistake, but I'd suggest putting these solutions aside for later consideration and taking a more structured approach. Here is the process I suggest you follow:

- Deal with each performance objective on its own, and think about the best way to teach that one objective.

- Look for patterns that emerge as you go through the list of objectives, and visualize how you might deliver on the emerging instructional strategy.

- Use your measurement strategy to visualize how a learner must perform the task. Once you can see the measurement, you can more easily determine how to teach the task.

It's very difficult to separate delivery system selection, sometimes called media selection, from strategy selection. Based on my experience, you should focus on what has to take place and then determine what types of delivery systems can make that event or learning activity happen.

▶ Compliance Example

Many organizations in the banking, healthcare, pharmaceutical, and nuclear power industries have requirements for compliance training. The training usually includes a knowledge component and a behavioral component. A learner must know the regulations and be able to recognize when a particular regulation must be applied to a work situation. The learner must also be able to determine the correct action to take to remain in compliance and then take any appropriate action based on knowledge of the regulations to stay in compliance.

In this case, objectives that describe knowledge components require explanations, definitions, identification, and demonstrations. These instructional strategies can be delivered through e-learning or in a virtual classroom and measured through objective-type questions.

Using simulations or role-play scenarios is most appropriate for objectives that describe required actions based on knowledge of the regulations. This learning can be delivered in live or virtual classrooms or in some cases through e-learning. Measurement can be conducted by scoring simulations in an e-learning course or by live evaluators. Role plays can be measured by live evaluators using a checklist.

In order to deliver consistent business results, the critical links between the main task, objective, measurement strategy, and instructional strategy must be maintained. This is a technical example complete with industry jargon, but the objective clearly illustrates how this task should be measured and taught.

Main task: Prepare the valve operator for removal.

1. **Situation:** During a trip and throttle valve disassembly,

2. **Learned Capability:** the engineer will prepare

3. **Object:** the valve operator for removal

4. **Action:** by disengaging the trip hook from the latch-up lever, turning the valve operator handwheel counterclockwise to its stop, and moving the latch-up lever to its tripped position with the sliding nut just touching the surface of the valve stem coupling

5. **Tools/Constraints:** without jamming the latch-up lever.

   Measurement Strategy: Conduct a performance test observed by an evaluator with a checklist.

> **Instructional Strategy:** Provide structured demonstration on e-learning with animated graphics; provide an opportunity for practice on a sample valve operator in a lab with a facilitator.

◆ Getting Sign-Off on Your Objectives and Strategies

Before beginning the labor-intensive and time-consuming tasks of producing a final learning product, it is essential to gain consensus from the rest of your design team. With your measurement and instructional strategies determined, you have a logical, high-level design for your solution. Chapter 6 helps you take the output from the Analysis and Design phases into a blueprint meeting to get feedback from your team and gain consensus.

PLANNING FOR IMPLEMENTATION

The Design phase is the place to begin designing your implementation plan. This may be early in the project life cycle to begin thinking about implementation, but that's just the point. As Steven Covey says, "Begin with the end in mind." You will no doubt add more detail to your implementation plan and possibly make major changes to it before it is time to use it, but starting early will have everyone on the project team thinking about implementation, which ensures that it gets the proper amount of attention.

Organizational culture is often a make-or-break factor in the successful implementation of training. That's why it's so important to understand the existing culture and leverage that knowledge in such a way as to ensure that your client's learning and business goals are met.

◆ Four Implementation Categories

There are four major categories that you should include in your implementation planning:

Change management: The type of change management that I am talking about here is a potential change in the learning culture. There may be an organizational change management associated with your project, but that will have its own initiatives and implementation plans developed by another team. Training should be a part of the change management plan, and it should be integrated to achieve a consistent outcome.

An example of a change initiative that would affect the learning culture is the introduction of a new learning delivery system, such as m-learning. The learning culture analysis and delivery systems analysis will assist you in making decisions regarding change management issues related to the learning culture. Chapter 12 includes examples of these.

Timeline: Developing a timeline sounds simple enough, and in many cases it is as simple as determining when an e-learning course will be available for use. In the case of a blended learning solution that affects thousands of learners, it can be both complex and critical. If you are relying on technology, you must make plans well in advance to schedule technical support resources, which will likely include a learning management system. There are many activities to be scheduled in a blended learning solution, including possible classroom and instructor time. As you can see, depending on your solution, this step can be simple or it can get complicated.

Resources: A lot of different things can fall under the category of resources needed for a successful implementation. You may need people in the role of instructors or coaches, technology in the form of smart phones or tablets, or classroom facilities. Any number of other resources outside of your team may be needed to successfully implement your solution. Your implementation will go more smoothly if you think of these resources and begin planning for them early on, rather than waiting until the last minute.

Logistics: There are so many things that could fall under the category of logistics. Here are some examples:

- *For instructor-led training:* Ordering and shipping computers to training rooms, cleaning and setting up those rooms, ordering lunch, sending invitations or reminders to participants.

- *For e-learning:* Getting courses loaded on the LMS, setting up learner groups on the LMS, maybe configuring hardware or shipping headphones to people.

- *For performance support:* Making job aids available by e-mail or by providing laminated hard copies, providing support for replacement of lost job aids, testing all delivery devices for compatibility and screen size.

◈ Measuring Business Impact and Return on Investment

The Design phase is the time and place to plan for measuring results and possibly calculating the return on investment from your project. As with many steps in this flexible model, you won't do this for every project. Measurement of learning takes place as learners proceed with the learning materials, but measurement of results and ROI take place after implementation.

Measurement of results is the basis for making your new instructional design process sustainable. You and your team will gain support for doing things differently in your design process by proving that the results are worth the effort. The strategy of leveraging ROI to make the Handshaw Instructional Design Model sustainable is discussed in detail in Chapter 13.

THE NEXT PHASE . . .

By now, you can appreciate the role that performance objectives play in your design and that they are useful as more than just advanced organizers for learners. You can see that performance objectives rely on the foundation of a good task analysis and that they not only define the measurement strategy but ultimately define the instructional strategy. Before you begin to use your measurement strategies, instructional strategies, and culture and implementation plans, it is important to get buy-in from your client and the rest of your design team. Chapter 6 introduces the blueprint meeting, which helps you build valuable consensus.

The Blueprint Meeting

With the Analysis and Design phases completed, it's time to get busy creating content. But here are two questions to consider before moving on: Are you sure the entire design team is on board with your recommendations? And are you confident that your sponsor or client won't second-guess your finished project once the project is delivered? The blueprint meeting (see Figure 6.1) is designed to bring your entire team into alignment and gain consensus for the completion of your recommended solutions. You won't find this step in the traditional ADDIE model, but I believe it's critical to the success of any design project. Taking the time to have this structured meeting ensures that all the stakeholders fully agree on

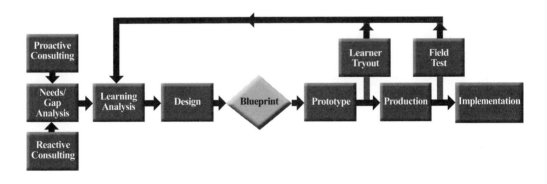

FIGURE 6.1 Handshaw Instructional Design Model: Blueprint Meeting

the expected goals, objectives, and business outcomes reflected in the content of your final training design.

THE NEED FOR ALIGNMENT

The blueprint meeting is another part of the Handshaw process that came about as a direct result of working with a client. This particular client used a team meeting to ensure alignment among a large internal team and several external project partners. The approach is particularly useful in organizations that operate in silos and helps prevent client disappointments and costly rework. You won't use the blueprint meeting with every project, but you can use it on larger projects or where there is a need for alignment. You can apply the cost-vs.-risk rule to determine when you need a blueprint meeting.

▶ Blueprint Meeting Example

Our client had six executive presidents, each of whom was responsible for a line of business. They all had to agree on the redesign of an enterprise-wide manager training program. Each line of business had its own group of subject matter experts, which included other external partners. Our analysis and design work set the measurement and instructional strategies for the entire project, so getting consensus and sign-off was crucial. Our client pulled together the entire team for a meeting, which we designed and called a *blueprint meeting*. This experience led to the creation of a new and valuable part of our process.

The meeting lasted three hours. We began it by presenting the results of our analysis. Unfortunately, the business executives quickly became bored with our analysis data. The meeting could have been better and shorter had we led with our measurement strategy and our instructional strategy. Now we always begin our meetings with what the executives want to know: "What are you going to do for me?"

As we presented our measurement and instructional strategies, the audience became more engaged and began to understand the purpose of the meeting. When design decisions were challenged, we referred to our analysis data for explanations and justification. Sometimes we were met with consensus and sometimes we were met with requests for further explanations. At this point, helpful discussions led to revisions to the strategy that everyone could agree upon. The important outcome of the meeting was that we reached consensus on the high-level results for the project. It was especially important for the executives from each line of business to agree on the measurement strategy, which led to a higher-level plan for accountability.

By gaining consensus for measurement and instructional strategies in a blueprint meeting, you will spend less time making sweeping changes during your content development. The people who need to attend this meeting are those true clients you talked to in the performance consulting and Gaps Map meetings. It may take you some time and convincing to set up a blueprint meeting, but you will find it worth the effort.

Be sure to apply the cost-vs.-risk rule when you are deciding whether you should invest the time and effort in a blueprint meeting. If you have a small team who has already seen all of your analysis and design documents and signed off on them, you may not need a meeting to gain consensus. On occasion, however, there is value in getting even a small team together to make sure everyone understands your plan before you begin development.

If you have a large team representing multiple lines of business, a high-cost project, or a change initiative, you should conduct a blueprint meeting. Plan ahead. Don't wait until your deliverables for the meeting are finished. Plan to hold the meeting a week or so after everyone has received your measurement and instructional strategy documents.

PREPARING FOR THE BLUEPRINT MEETING

Once you have decided that a blueprint meeting is necessary to make sure everyone has really read and understood your analysis and design documents, you need to do a little preparation.

▶ Agenda

Start by preparing your agenda. Begin with introductions, including each person's role on the project team. The next item on your agenda should be a review of project activities up to this point. Proceed to a review of your process and the importance of the meeting in achieving the desired business outcomes. A prominent agenda item for the meeting should be setting the tone for the meeting by clearly stating the business goal and making sure everyone is focused on achieving that goal.

In order to keep everyone engaged, move quickly to your recommendations for measurement and instructional strategies. This is the main agenda item for your meeting, so be sure to give it enough time. It is difficult to gauge how much pushback you may get as you go through this section. If this portion of the meeting doesn't go as long as you thought, you can always finish early. The last portion of the meeting should deal with agreed-upon revisions and next steps. Notice that this sample agenda is short and simple (Figure 6.2). Notice also the recommended times. These are only estimates and you may not be able to stick to them, but they can help guide expectations.

▶ Deliverables

There are only three required deliverables for most blueprint meetings:

1. Measurement strategy
2. Instructional strategy
3. Content outline

Agenda

1. Introduction of all team members (15 minutes)
2. Recap analysis and design phases (15 minutes)
3. Review of desired business outcomes (10 minutes)
4. Measurement recommendations (30 minutes)
5. Instructional strategy recommendations (30 minutes)
6. Review solution and agreed-upon revisions (30 minutes)
7. Discuss next steps (15 minutes)

FIGURE 6.2   Blueprint Meeting Agenda Example

Start with your measurement strategy and then present your instructional strategy. A high-level—not detailed—content outline provides your audience with a comfort level. Be sure you give people enough time to read your deliverables. Use graphics or flowcharts in order to keep text to a minimum. Your stakeholders and sponsors just want to know what you plan to do. It is better to give them less information and have them read and understand your strategies than to give them so much that they become confused or disengaged.

If your strategy is new or perhaps difficult for the participants to visualize, you might consider developing a prototype for your blueprint meeting. This may require some additional preparation time, but it just might save your blueprint meeting. No matter how clear your description of your strategy might seem to you, a good example in the form of a prototype can be worth well over a thousand words. Even if your prototype isn't perfect, it adds excitement and clarity to the meeting.

▶ Selecting and Preparing a Prototype

Finally, if you are considering including a prototype in your meeting, use the cost-vs.-risk rule again. Pick out a portion of the instruction that best exemplifies your strategies, and develop that portion for the meeting (see Figure 6.3). If you do this, don't invest an inordinate amount of time in case your strategy must be radically changed as a result of the meeting. Use of prototypes is discussed further in Chapter 7.

CONDUCTING THE BLUEPRINT MEETING

Explain your agenda to everyone, and then do your best to follow it. Think back to your performance consulting meetings, where your job was to ask a few good questions and then listen. The purpose of this meeting is to explain how the strategy for your learning solution will help support the achievement of the business goal and then listen to your stakeholders' and experts' opinions. You can use drawings on a whiteboard or handouts. If you choose to use PowerPoint slides, be careful how you use them. The overuse of slides puts people in a listening mode, which puts you in a telling mode. Remember, this meeting is all about your listening in order to gain consensus.

You are conducting this meeting to verify your strategy, to make sure your strategy is correct and that it supports achievement of the stated business goal. You are not here to sell your strategy. As you elicit opinions from attendees, you should separate opinions from facts. You have analysis data upon which your strategies are based, so refer to this data. If the analysis data turns

Instructional Strategy

Conceptual Information
The course will be designed with as much interactivity as possible while conveying conceptual information about Service Leader tasks to learners. High-level notes on conceptual information will be included in the Participant Guides, along with space for notes. Conceptual information will be recalled and used during activities. Some system screen shots may also be included for later reference.

Demonstrations
During the course, the facilitator will demonstrate the completion of some tasks in the system. Whether in a small group setting or a larger classroom, the facilitator can project his or her computer screen to show how to pull specific information and run example reports. While some screen shots may be included in course materials for later reference, we recommend that the facilitator complete demonstrations in the live system whenever possible to help learners become comfortable with navigating through the system. Participant Guides will include a space for demonstration notes.

Interactivity
As previously mentioned, the course will be designed with as much interactivity as possible. This will largely take a group discussion format in which the facilitator asks learners to share their thoughts and experiences as tasks are taught. Facilitators will ask learners to share their on-the-job experiences, which have proven to be very valuable for other learners.

The course will also include structured activities, which, depending on the size of the class, may be small group breakout activities or simply a group discussion. For example, the course may include activities to have learners review a "case study" or scenario describing a typical situation that a Service Leader must handle and asking learners to answer questions about how he or she might respond to the demands of the job to complete tasks.

Job Aids
The Participant Guide will include some reference information that learners can use on the job after class. In particular, the guide will include a checklist of daily and weekly tasks that learners can copy and use if they find it helpful. Other such tools may be developed during the production of the course materials.

Measurement Strategy

We recommend the use of low-tech and easy-to-use performance tests to measure the actual outcomes of using the system. Learners will be given access to the system and asked to complete a series of fill-in-the-blank questions. Sample tasks for the exercises would

(continues)

be to report on equipment status, part order status, or even to run reports and answer key questions with them.

The performance test design will simulate actual on-the-job use of the system and give learners valuable practice and build confidence for using the system to solve problems in day-to-day use.

Course Outline

Instructor-Led Training

	Module	Time Estimate	Topics
1	Course Introduction	20 minutes	• Flex and stretch • Course intro and objectives • Agenda for the day • Icebreaker activity
2	The Service Leader Role	30 minutes	• Service Leader qualities • Service Leader goals • Safety overview • Service Leader responsibilities • Managing technicians • Managing your time
3	Managing Your Day	20 minutes	• Conducting daily huddles • Performing yard walks • Planning and adjusting tasks • Delegating tasks
4	Overview	1 hour	• Overview of how you use Wynne • Walkthrough of the Wynne 7.11 screen • Overview of other reports/information

FIGURE 6.3   Blueprint Meeting Measurement and Instructional Strategy with Content Outline

out to be wrong or incomplete, take time in this meeting to correct the data if you can. If you can't gain consensus right away, table the issue for later. Just make sure you have identified the appropriate individuals to help you correct or complete the data so you can revise and verify your strategies later.

If you decide to use a prototype in your meeting, explain your measurement and instructional strategies first, then use the prototype as a demonstration. This is a good time to explain how you plan to test the prototype with sample learners. Since these tests may require three to four hours of an employee's time, you might also take the opportunity to solicit support for this testing time from stakeholders.

▶ Identifying Next Steps

It is critical to capture your next steps at the conclusion of your meeting. Don't get caught in discussions so long that you don't have time to summarize their outcomes. This is a consensus-gaining meeting, so try to list all agreed-upon changes at the conclusion of the meeting. Be sure to list everything that was agreed upon, especially the things that did not change.

ANALYZING AND USING BLUEPRINT RESULTS

Once you complete the blueprint meeting and record the results, including all the points of agreement and all the requested changes, you need to meet with your design team to analyze and implement the results. This should be a small and informal meeting that includes just your immediate design team and possibly one or two trusted subject matter experts. If you are a team of one, try to include someone from the client side to go over your results with you.

During your blueprint meeting you probably collected lots of opinions, learned a few useful or new facts, and found many areas of agreement and a few areas of disagreement. You have just one more short validation step to go before you begin the Production phase, where you will expend most of your project resources and time.

Note that even at this stage there may still be some members of your design team who disagree with your solution. If this is the case, enlist their help during the Learner Tryout phase with a prototype to gather additional data to support your design.

THE NEXT PHASE . . .

You have reached an important milestone in your instructional design process. You have made decisions about measurement and instructional strategies based on solid analysis data, and you have gained consensus from your client, stakeholders, and project team. There is one very important stakeholder who can help you validate your strategies and give you valuable feedback: your learner. In the next phase, you will learn how to select and test a prototype with sample learners. Input from the learner audience provides you with some of the best design advice you can find—for free.

CHAPTER 7

Validate Your Strategies with a Prototype

At this point in your design process, you should develop and test a prototype because you don't know yet whether the measurement and instructional strategies will help your learners master the performance objectives. Your design will remain a prototype until you have proven to yourself and your client that it actually does what it is intended to do.

This chapter shows you how to build a prototype. It also explains the Learner Tryout phase of the design process (Figure 7.1) and shows you why formative evaluation is like an insurance policy for instructional design.

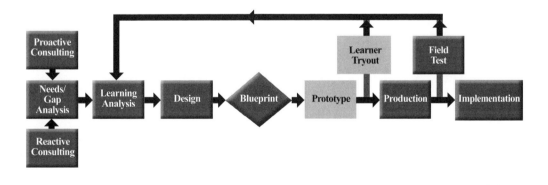

FIGURE 7.1   Handshaw Instructional Design Model: Prototype

LEARNERS ARE YOUR BEST DESIGN CONSULTANTS

It's an ironic fact of life that most organizations completely ignore the best and most informed instructional design consultants in the world—their learners. Just think about all the training you have experienced in your life, and consider all the suggestions you might have given if someone had bothered to ask you about your experience. If there were gaps or problems with the training, you probably had an opinion about what would make the training more useful to you. Learners can provide you with good feedback about what would make training more useful to them.

In our experience, when we've asked our clients for permission to conduct a learner tryout, we've often received pushback. Not taking the time to do things right the first time is becoming a recurring theme in this book. Your best shot at overcoming this client objection is to point out to your client the risk of deploying an untested design to hundreds or even thousands of learners. Once your client considers the cost of ineffective training, the idea of getting feedback from a handful of learners before developing and implementing the final training program is an easier sell to make.

You should also explain to your client that there is a difference between getting feedback from subject matter experts and getting it from actual learners. SMEs can comment on the completeness and accuracy of the content, but they are not equipped to comment on whether people can actually learn from the training. Actual learners have a unique perspective. They can tell you whether the information is clear and logical or whether interactive exercises are useful and relevant. They can even tell you whether one strategy works better than another.

WHY GUESS WHEN YOU CAN MEASURE?

Few people will argue with the results of learner feedback gathered in a controlled testing environment. But when issues of disagreement or uncertainty arise, there is no need to guess what the correct course of action is when you can measure.

It's important to understand the difference between *formative evaluation* and *summative evaluation*. Dr. Robert Stake, who has written extensively about formative evaluation, offers a wonderful definition for both types of evaluation: "When the cook tastes the soup, that's formative; when the guests taste the soup, that's summative." Sivasailam Thiagarajan, Ph.d., known as Thiagi, has a definition that highlights his trademark sense of humor and talent for creating memorable quips: "Formative is to improve; and summative is to prove."

Stake suggests two levels of formative evaluation. He calls the first level a *learner tryout*. This is an informal test of a prototype of a learning solution conducted with a small group of learners. The purpose of this informal test is to verify that the instructional strategy enables learners to master the learning objectives.

Stake calls the second level a *field test*. This is a more formal test of the entire learning solution under conditions that simulate the real learning environment as closely as possible. The clear goal of both of these tests is to measure the success of the learning design and implementation, not that of the learners taking the test. Both tests generate data used for improving the learning solution until the learners are able to demonstrate mastery of the learning objectives.

▶ Cost-vs.-Risk Rule

Whether you should conduct a learner tryout at this point can be determined by applying the cost-vs.-risk rule again. If you are recommending a new strategy, you need a tryout. Even if the strategy is not new, but there were people in the blueprint meeting who were not completely in agreement with your measurement or instructional strategies, a learner tryout will prove the point one way or another. If the training program is being designed for a very large audience, there is also risk involved, which indicates that it is worth the time to conduct a learner tryout.

Here are several benefits from conducting a learner tryout that you can put into the "benefit" column of your cost-vs.-risk comparison:

- You can collect objective data while observing the learner completing the tryout by asking the learner to "think out loud" as he or she proceeds in either a self-paced e-learning course or an instructor-led course.

- You can test the validity and reliability of your measurement strategy. If any of your testing instruments aren't working, you have an opportunity to find out why and make necessary revisions.

- You can ask learners for suggestions for ways to improve any deficiencies that you discover.

- If your design team disagrees about the best instructional strategy to use, you can test multiple strategies to measure which one works best.

- When you ask learners to be involved in the design and development of their learning solutions and then listen to their ideas and advice, you establish great allies with a positive attitude.

Don't overlook this last benefit of gaining support from your learners. Even well-designed learning solutions don't deliver results if learners are not engaged. When you involve learners in their own learning program design, you gain valuable allies in promoting the value of the program to others. This intangible benefit alone can make it worth your while to conduct a learner tryout. The following example illustrates this point.

One of our clients was preparing to implement a new commercial loan system. Once we developed measurement and instructional strategies for the system, we created a prototype and conducted a learner tryout. As a result of the learner tryout, our client was relieved to find out that the team really liked the new system and the training. Everyone was pleased that we conducted a learner tryout, which created a positive attitude toward not only the training, but the new system.

CONDUCTING THE LEARNER TRYOUT

The secret to a successful learner tryout is in the preparation. The first task is to select the appropriate content to include in the prototype and choose the right participants as sample learners. Then you need to prepare the prototype, the learners, the facilities, and the test facilitators. Conducting the test is relatively quick and easy, but it does require some specific practices. Once you have collected the data correctly, analyzing it and making decisions about revisions are a fairly straightforward process.

▶ Selecting and Developing a Prototype

Developing a prototype for a learner tryout does not require any additional work. Begin the process by selecting a portion of your instructional design that best exemplifies your agreed-upon instructional and measurement strategies. The delivery system doesn't matter. You can conduct a learner tryout for a virtual classroom, for instructor-led situations, for m-learning (learning delivered by mobile phones or tablets), or for e-learning.

Use the cost-vs.-risk rule to select the appropriate modules for prototype development and testing. If one module of an e-learning course represents the new or risky part of your instructional strategy, then develop that twenty-minute module of instruction for the learner tryout. With a more elaborate strategy, you may not be able to test your entire instructional strategy with one twenty-minute module. You may have to develop more than one module of instruction to collect conclusive data for your entire strategy.

I recommend that you put the least amount of work into the finished prototype product that you can and still have it function the way you want it to. Don't agonize over high-quality graphics or expensive video production with professional talent. Use low production values as long as their use does not interfere with the learning experience or impact the credibility of your training department or company. If you're too invested in an expensive prototype, you might resist making changes if the prototype fails. Failure is a perfectly acceptable outcome of a learner tryout. Weigh all these factors to decide how much effort should go into developing your prototype.

➤ Preparing for the Learner Tryout

The following is a suggested list of tasks to consider when preparing for a learner tryout. You may not need everything on this list, or you may need to add steps of your own.

- **Review the instruction:** Review the instructional materials to better understand what needs to be measured, and list any specific issues for which you need more data. If you have differences of opinion or there are specific items that you have questions about, design the test to make sure you get data to resolve those issues. You can design and test multiple scenarios to see which ones work best. You can ask questions of the learners if you need feedback in specific areas. This is your opportunity to make the test work for you.

- **Customize the checklists and interview sheets:** Checklists are used by learners and observers to record learner comments. Interview sheets are used by observers to record answers to pre- and postinterview questions. Develop templates for checklists and interview sheets that you can customize to meet the needs of each tryout.

■ **Select the learners:** Select at least six learners for your tryout. Be sure to select learners who represent all facets of the audience as defined by your audience analysis. Include, for example, new hires, experienced people, and novices. Learners are people who need to learn and have no prior knowledge of the content. Subject matter experts who helped you create the learning do not count as sample learners.

■ **Train the coaches and observers:** Coaches are SMEs who are able to coach the learners through the training if the prototype fails, especially in self-paced learning. Observers are there to record data and help conduct the learning, but they do not impart any content knowledge to learners. Coaches and observers should practice completing the checklists and conducting interviews while someone plays the role of a learner. This rehearsal ensures that the entire team is ready for the first group of sample learners. Once your coaches have experience conducting learner tryouts, you can skip this training step.

■ **Develop the agenda:** Once you have done a quick run-through of the steps required to complete the tryout, you can more accurately estimate the time needed for preparing sample learners, conducting the test, and collecting data.

■ **Design the facility layout:** Make sure you have enough room and equipment for all participants. Decide where the equipment will go and where observers and coaches will sit. This is especially important for e-learning and m-learning situations.

■ **Set up and test the facilities:** Two days before the tryout is to begin, you should set up and test all equipment and/or classroom facilities according to your facility layout plan. Equipment and facilities may include a computer for e-learning, a tablet for m-learning, or a classroom for instructor-led training.

◆ Conducting the Learner Tryout

- **Prepare the subjects:** Inform all learners of the purpose of the tryout and the important role they will play. Reassure the learners that you are not testing them. Make it clear that their purpose is to test the training materials and program design to ensure that they meet the stated goals. If appropriate, conduct a pretryout interview to record any pretraining attitudes that may exist.

- **Implement preparatory training:** If the prototype you chose for the tryout is in the middle or near the end of the course, you'll need to get your sample learners caught up on the part of the course they missed. This can easily be done with a short instructor-led training session. Failure to provide this training will invalidate your tryout.

- **Conduct the tryout:** The best data results are achieved when one observer works with one learner at a time. That might seem like a lot of attention, but you only need to conduct this tryout six times, so it's not an extraordinary time commitment. If you have two observers conduct the tryout in separate rooms, it might be possible to gather the data in less time. Make coaches available to help the learners when they don't know how to proceed. This allows the observers to concentrate on recording data.

- **Observe and complete the checklists:** While the test is being conducted, observers should complete the customized checklists and take notes. Observers should avoid jumping in to coach or help learners so that failures are allowed to happen. Provide the least amount of instruction possible, and then make revisions only when the instructional strategy fails. This yields the most efficient instruction, without adding more instruction than learners need.

■ **Conduct interviews:** After the test is completed, observers should conduct interviews using the customized posttest interview sheets. This is helpful for anecdotal data or measuring changes in attitudes.

◈ Analyzing Data from the Learner Tryout

■ **Compile the data from the checklists:** Review all the data collected, and compile the results. The tryout may produce two checklists from each learner. Some learners may write their comments on checklists themselves, while others may wish to provide comments verbally so they can be recorded by observers. Either way, the data will reveal definite trends about the training.

■ **Compile the data from the interview sheets:** If you choose to conduct pre- or posttryout interviews, you can gather data to help answer specific questions you and your team have about different elements of the training. Data from interviews may be more opinion-based and attitudinal in nature, but it too will help you make better design decisions.

■ **Determine needed revisions:** You shouldn't make every change suggested by one or two learners, but you will quickly be able to identify strong trends, which will point to the needed revisions.

This section summarizes trends observed during the learner tryout and recommended actions in response to each trend.

#	Observed Trend	Recommendations	Decision
1	The hands-on practice instructions are detailed and complicated.	• We recommend adding an accompanying PowerPoint to summarize the hands-on practice instructions. This will help the learners follow along and also ensure that the instructor hits all the key points that learners need to know about the simulations. • Also, some clarification is needed on the trainer's role during the hands-on practice. Instructions should more clearly introduce the observational coaching concept.	Add both the PowerPoint slides for the instructions and clarification on the instructor's role.
2	The hands-on practice demonstration requires some improvement.	• The instructor's typical process is to describe some basics about the screens during the demonstration. This was not in the Leader's Guide for this class. Should a conceptual overview be added to the content? • Ensure that cash counting is part of the demo. • Ensure that the checklists and appropriate debriefing are included in the demo. • Add an example of typing incorrectly in the demo. • Consider adding a referral opportunity to the demo.	• Add an extra section to the ILT for a system overview. This should be separate from the demonstration and come before it. Add a section in the Screen Guide for this overview. • ILT will introduce free-form referral opportunities at a high level. The Leader's Guide should include notes to remind learners that they will learn more about referrals during postwork and coaching in the branch.
3	Observers were concerned that cash counting methods were not being followed.	Cash counting methods had not yet been taught to learners. The section on cash counting will remain in the first day of the ILT class. Cash counting should also be added to the demonstration. Consider adding cash counting to the performance checklist, as well.	Cash counting will not be added to the checklist.
4	The pacing of the transactions seemed appropriate. The first transaction took a bit longer while learners got acclimated to the activity. Transaction times averaged about 15 minutes each. Feedback from both the participants and instructor indicated the timing was on target.	• Add more time for the first transaction in round 1. • Let's discuss the feedback on the timing and evaluate our estimates.	We all agree that the pacing of the transactions is appropriate. We will continue to use 7–8 minutes per transaction (15 minutes for both partners to complete one transaction).

FIGURE 7.2 Learner Tryout Data and Recommended Revisions Example

◆ Making Revisions with Consensus

Learner tryout results yield good data from which to make decisions about revisions. Not all your decisions will be supported by data, so you may have to make some judgment calls as you decide what to do with your prototype and future modules of instruction. The payoff of time and money saved comes from catching problems with your learning solutions early in the process so you don't repeat those mistakes in future modules. It is easier to make changes to a quickly produced prototype than to an entire course.

If you are working with a small team interpreting the results from a tryout for a short piece of instruction, you can meet with your design team or a subject matter expert and review the data once it is analyzed. Keep in mind that you need to make decisions based on data trends. Remember, you can't please everyone, or you would be in a constant state of revision.

If you are part of a large team with many different opinions being represented, you will have to take a more collaborative and more time-consuming approach to identifying revisions. In this case, you may need to produce a written report that summarizes your data and makes written recommendations. Having a face-to-face meeting to review the report is a good way to proceed once you distribute the data and written recommendations.

The most important point to consider when making design decisions from the data produced by a learner tryout is that data always speaks louder than opinions. To get a better understanding of how this works, see Figure 7.2, which shows the partial results from an actual learner tryout along with the recommended design decisions.

The next time you are stymied about a design idea, whether you are unsure about your own idea or you are questioning your client's ideas, consider a learner tryout. Why guess when you can measure?

THE NEXT PHASE . . .

The Production phase comes next in the Handshaw Instructional Design Model and is the most time consuming and expensive phase. In the Production phase, you create all the instructional materials for instructor-led training, virtual classrooms, e-learning, performance support, or m-learning. You will appreciate the fact that the formative evaluation "insurance policy" you purchased during this Prototype phase saves you countless hours of revisions during the Production phase.

CHAPTER 8

Designing for the Classroom–
Virtual and Live

The Production phase (Figure 8.1) is the most expensive and time-consuming phase of the instructional design process because it's the part in which detailed content is developed. All the work you've completed leading up to this phase of the model—from needs/gap analysis, through learning analysis, design, and the blueprint meeting to prototype creation—culminates with the creation of a detailed content outline.

By the time you get to the Production phase, you know with certainty that any content created during this phase will align with your client's or the

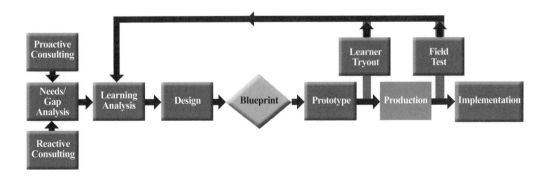

FIGURE 8.1   Handshaw Instructional Design Model: Production

organization's business goals. All that work you did prior to this phase keeps you from having to make costly revisions to your content.

PRACTICE AND FEEDBACK—WHAT LEARNERS NEED MOST

What learners need in order to perform is practice and feedback, so don't miss any opportunity you're given to use this valuable training tool. Giving your learners a "death by PowerPoint" one-way classroom experience is not an efficient use of classroom time, nor is it the best way to present knowledge to learners. Instead, use learning technologies such as e-learning and m-learning to provide content knowledge. Once you have provided instruction for knowledge objectives (remember the knowledge steps in your task analysis?), you can maximize your classroom time by providing lots of practice and feedback.

Assuming you correctly selected classroom or virtual learning for skill building in your instructional strategy, the primary training content deliverables are the Participant's Guide and the Facilitator's Guide. Here's how to build both of these essential documents, along with some experience-based tips and tools to help move the creation process along.

THE PARTICIPANT'S GUIDE

The Participant's Guide should be light on content and heavy on instructions for classroom activities.

Brevity is the most important rule to remember when creating a Participant's Guide. In fact, one of our most experienced instructional designers puts it this way: "Decide how much content you think you'll need and then cut that in half." Remember—you're creating a guide, not supplemental classroom reading for your learners. You don't want your learners reading the guide during class; you want them engaged in what's going on.

As noted earlier, a blended solution that uses e-learning or m-learning is an efficient way to provide the knowledge needed to meet your content objectives. If class size or other technical or resource limitations prevent such a solution, you'll have to incorporate this content in the classroom design.

Although you need to include content in your Participant's Guide, avoid copying your PowerPoint slides into your guide. The information that is presented in class should be distilled in your guide (see Figure 8.2). Your learners should be focused on the instructor and on participating in classroom events, which improves the retention of the information being presented.

Real learning occurs when practice and feedback exercises are provided in your instructional design. Keep the informational portion of the training as brief as possible, and focus your work on including more engaging and interactive content for your learners.

▶ Simulation and Role Play

Conducting a simulation or role play in class is one of the best ways to provide practice. The accompanying feedback component is where most of the critical learning takes place. Think about yourself as a learner. It may be fairly straightforward to think you can do something by watching a demonstration but quite another matter when you actually have to perform the task yourself. Once you practice and receive feedback and coaching, you begin to own the behavior.

The attitude change that accompanies classroom activities is a key benefit of role plays, simulations, and simulation games. Many managers think the sign of a successful training event is that everyone does well in class and heads back to work. In order to achieve business results, you need more than a good classroom experience with favorable instructor evaluations. Your learners need to be able to perform at the level required to achieve business results. More important, they must also choose to perform those behaviors every day on the job. Part of choosing the learned behavior comes from confidence, which you must build through experience and feedback. Delivering instructor-led train-

Module 3—Managing Your Day

Section Overview   This module describes how you can best manage your day in order to accomplish your tasks.

Section Objectives   After completing this module, you will be able to:
- Conduct daily huddles
- Perform yard walks
- Plan, adjust, and delegate tasks

Conducting Daily Huddles

During the daily huddle, you should accomplish the following:
- Flex-and-stretch
- Safety discussion

Performing Yard Walks

During yard walks, you should accomplish the following:
- Identify and immediately correct safety hazards
- Verify that equipment is properly tagged
- Verify that equipment is in the proper area of the yard
- Perform QC of equipment
- Identify out-of-service units
- Inspect units for up-to-date annual inspection performance and date stamps
- Discuss rental flow and housekeeping concerns with the CSR

Performing daily huddles and yard walks in the morning gives you visibility into the current state of the yard and shop and the work to be done. You should use this information to plan your day, prioritizing and delegating as needed.

 Activity: Managing Your Day

Your instructor will ask you questions about the following scenario:

During his first yard walk of the day, Joe notices the following:
- There are four pieces of equipment in the To Be Readied for Rent area of the yard
- Two pieces of equipment are in the To Be Repaired area of the yard
- One of the pieces of equipment in the Ready to Rent area is tagged improperly
- One boom lift requires an annual inspection

Notes

FIGURE 8.2   Sample Participant's Guide

ing is time consuming and expensive, so you must do more than just present information. You have to build skills, build confidence, and change attitudes if you want to get measurable results from the learner experience.

▶ Testing

Your Participant's Guide should also contain instructions and scoring criteria for testing. Including some sort of measurement in the classroom is another way to say to everyone that you expect to get results out of your efforts. The degree to which classroom activities should be formally scored can be determined by culture and individual situations.

The Handshaw model assumes the selection of a testing instrument based on performance objectives. The model also assumes that you'll pair a classroom activity with a specific measurement exercise so that the test is an extension of classroom activity up to that point. Learners, their managers, and the facilitators benefit from this process because the test is a valid testing instrument that is directly relevant or useful to the job. Feedback, coupled with a mastery test that identifies areas for improvement, increases the likelihood that new learned behaviors will be applied on the job. So make sure you include any performance test you design along with testing instructions and scoring criteria in the Participant's Guide.

▶ Performance Support

Providing *performance support*—also referred to as *job aids* or *electronic performance support*—is a good way to ensure that performance in the classroom transfers to performance on the job. It doesn't make sense to require performers to memorize a list of procedural detail if the information can be accessed at the moment it's needed to perform a task. Performance support is the ultimate use of context to link training to performance.

There is one more thing you may wish to include in your Participant's Guide. If you choose to provide an advanced organizer for your learners, include the performance objectives. If they are long and unwieldy, do a little editing to make them more user-friendly. Remember: The shorter they are, the better your chances they will actually be read.

To summarize, your Participant's Guide needs to provide guidance for classroom activities, provide a minimum of content to support those activities, and be useful for a refresher or reference.

THE FACILITATOR'S GUIDE

A Facilitator's Guide ensures consistent learning results no matter who ultimately facilitates your training design. In smaller teams the designer and the facilitator might be the same person, but in larger teams you'll have to rely on other instructors to deliver the classroom instruction. The Facilitator's Guide becomes the key to being able to ensure consistent results.

Set the tone for consistency and quality of outcomes for your facilitators by including your performance objectives on the first page of your Facilitator's Guide. Not only do the objectives describe to facilitators what learners must be able to do, they also describe exactly how learners must perform and to what degree of proficiency.

Determine how much detail is appropriate by applying the cost-vs.-risk rule. If the facilitators are not subject matter experts, include more content. If you expect them to be knowledgeable SMEs, include less content.

You need to know the skills and attitudes of your facilitators. Since you are producing a guide for their use, you should conduct an audience analysis, just as you did with your learners.

➡ Experienced Facilitators, Knowledgeable SMEs

If your instructors know the content and are experienced facilitators, your job is easy. Make sure they have clear instructions for classroom activities and a timeline for the events of the class. A timeline is particularly important, since knowledgeable SMEs tend to focus on content and not on student experience, coaching, and feedback. The content-heavy focus reduces the business and performance impact of the training. Figure 8.3 is an example taken from a Facilitator's Guide for knowledgeable SMEs who are experienced facilitators.

▶ Experienced Facilitators, Less Knowledgeable SMEs

If your instructors are not knowledgeable on content but are experienced facilitators, you have to include more content, with less structure for how to provide coaching and feedback. Keep instructors focused on facilitating classroom activities and not on content delivery. If your facilitators are not subject matter experts, you need to make sure the content delivery portion of your instructional strategy is effective. Include a mastery test at the conclusion of the content presentation to ensure that your learners have mastered the knowledge components before they attempt the time-consuming classroom activities.

Think about your task analysis and the hierarchical task analysis example (see Figure 4.3). Learners must be able to master basic knowledge before they can master more advanced knowledge, which is essential for them to be able to complete a knowledge goal.

Figure 8.4 is an example of a Facilitator's Guide written for experienced facilitators with low content knowledge.

▶ Less Experienced Facilitator, Knowledgeable SME

Strong subject matter experts with little expertise as facilitators can be a challenging group. You will need a good Facilitator's Guide and a good train-the-trainer program. You should include content even though your facilitators are well-versed in content. The goal is for your facilitators to use the content you have selected and *only* the content you have selected.

Experienced SMEs want to tell your learners everything they know about the topic. This overloads your learners and does not leave enough time for

Module 6 – Processing a New Loan: Creating the Finance Request

Module Overview   In this module, you continue through the workflow for processing a new loan in the Commercial Lending system to create the finance request.

Module Objectives   After completing this module, you will be able to:

> Create a finance request in the Commercial Lending system by watching your trainer complete each step, then completing each step at your own workstation

Section 1—Creating the Finance Request

Time 2 hours

📖 **Refer** participants to Module 6, Section 1 on page 10 and Appendix B: Processing a New Loan on page 34 of their Participant Guide.

☐ **Activity: Creating the Finance Request Demonstration**

In this activity, demonstrate the steps for the second portion of the end-to-end new loan workflow in the Commercial Lending system—creating the finance request. Working with the SME, complete each step on the following pages, allowing participants to complete the same step at their workstations immediately following your demonstration of the step.

1. Complete the first step of the process for creating the finance request, instructing participants to watch as you complete the step.

2. After the participants watch you complete the first step, instruct the participants to complete the same step you just completed at their own workstations.

3. Follow the same demonstration guidelines that you did in Section 1 on page 18.

FIGURE 8.3   Facilitator's Guide for Knowledgeable SMEs with Facilitation Experience *(Note: The instructions are brief for both content and facilitation.)*

Module 5 – Processing a New Loan: Building the Customer Profile

Module Overview   In this module, you begin walking through the workflow for processing a new loan in the Commercial Lending system, beginning with building the customer profile.

Module Objectives   After completing this module, you will be able to:

> Build a customer profile for a new loan in the Commercial Lending system by watching your trainer complete each step, then completing each step at your own workstation

Section 1—Building the Customer Profile

Time 1 hour, 15 minutes

📖 **Refer** participants to Module 5, Section 1 on page 12 and Appendix B: Processing a New Loan on page 31 of their Participant Guide. Additionally, hand out copies of the Account Numbers and User IDs worksheet.

🗌 **Activity: Building the Customer Profile Demonstration**

In this activity, demonstrate the steps for the first portion of the end-to-end new loan workflow in the Commercial Lending system—building the customer profile. Working with the SME, complete each step on the following pages, allowing participants to complete the same step at their workstations immediately following your demonstration of the step.

1. If participants have not already logged on to their computers and the Commercial Lending training environment, have them do so now. To save time, you can ask participants to sign on as soon as they enter the classroom.

2. Access the Commercial Lending system and project it so the class can view your screen.

3. Read the following scenario information to the class. This information is also included in their Participant Guide so they can follow along.

4. Complete the first step of the process for building a customer profile, instructing participants to watch as you complete the step. Later in this section, you will find the following:
   - A step-by-step list of tasks you need to complete as you go through the demonstration
   - A high-level list of tasks in the workflow, including representative screen shots

---

FIGURE 8.4   Facilitator's Guide for Experienced Facilitators with Low Content Knowledge *(Note: Most of the instructions deal with content, not how to facilitate.)*

Module 1 – Getting Started: Day 1

Module Overview   This module will introduce you to Day 1 of the Commercial Lending system instructor-led training.

Module Objectives   After completing this module, you will be able to:

    Describe the purpose and goals of this course

Section 1—Ice Breaker

Time 30 minutes

📖 Materials

Flipchart

Markers

Sample drawings (use simple geometric examples)

☐ Activity

1. Ask for two volunteers.
2. Ask the volunteers to stand back-to-back, one facing a flipchart and one facing the group. The volunteer facing the flipchart is your illustrator and the volunteer facing the group is your leader.
3. Explain that the leader will be handed a piece of paper with a picture. The role of the guide is to give directions to the illustrator on how to replicate the drawing on the flipchart using only verbal cues.
4. Tell the illustrator to remain silent; he or she cannot ask questions.
5. Allow three minutes to accomplish this task.
6. Acknowledge your volunteers with a round of applause.

🗩 Ask

What was the most difficult part of this task?

How did this task make you feel?

What would make this task better?

🗣 Debrief

Communication and nonverbal cues are important even with routine and normal daily activities.

FIGURE 8.5 Facilitator's Guide for Knowledgeable SMEs with Little Facilitation Experience *(Note: Most of the instructions deal with how to facilitate and not with content knowledge.)*

learner practice and feedback. The best way to determine what is really needed is to consult your task analysis. If you include topics that are not on the task analysis, you are making the same mistakes as your SMEs. In addition, provide a detailed timeline with instructions for classroom activities with coaching and feedback. See the example in Figure 8.5.

▶ Train the Trainer

Even the best Facilitator's Guide won't guarantee consistent results unless facilitators practice their delivery and receive constructive feedback and coaching. Most trainers call this T3, or *train the trainer.* I prefer to think of it as "coaching the facilitator." In this case, your Facilitator's Guide becomes a performance support tool. Rather than lecturing your facilitators on the best practices of facilitation, you will achieve better results by asking each facilitator to conduct a portion of the course using the rest of the facilitator team as participants. By engaging the facilitator in learner experience with feedback, you accomplish two things at once: You provide the facilitator with the best possible learning experience, and you demonstrate that learner experience with practice and feedback is the most effective way to master a skill.

Make sure the class scheduling is done properly and that learners are notified of the commitment well in advance. Inform participants of the contents of the training class, and be sure they are given materials or assignments ahead of time.

INCORPORATING SOCIAL PRESENCE IN THE VIRTUAL CLASSROOM

Skill building is a primary reason you chose classroom delivery. Conducting role plays and simulations in the virtual classroom presents some creative challenges. In order to build skills and create this level of interactivity you have to use small groups and create a sense of *social presence.*

The researchers on social presence haven't reached agreement on a definition, so I'll give you mine. Social presence can approximate the types of intergroup communication that takes place in a face-to-face classroom. It also creates an awareness of other individuals in an online virtual classroom. I have found one magical and inexpensive tool that can accomplish this phenomenon: the webcam. Bandwidth becomes a barrier in terms of the number of individuals who can participate in a virtual classroom using webcams. Another factor is the number of faces you can keep up with on a screen, which is why we recommend small groups to make this to work. When you have a global audience in multiple time zones, even small groups in a virtual classroom are a less expensive and more convenient option than international travel.

◆ A Case Study Comparison

I recently had an opportunity to work with two clients in the same two-month period to help them improve their performance consulting skills. Both companies were global in scope, with participants in multiple time zones and of different nationalities. The training was delivered by virtual classroom, in two-hour sessions twice a week. The audiences were similar, and all training activities were identical, with one exception.

One client was able to use webcams for role-play activities, and the other client had no access to webcams. In both cases, class size was limited to only six participants. All six of the webcam users could see and hear each other. The participants without webcams could hear each other only during the role-play scenarios.

The group using the webcams during role plays performed very much like groups I have worked with in live classroom situations. Performance improves as learners gain practice and use more of the eight principles of performance consulting. The group that did not make use of the webcams did not improve performance as the role plays continued and reportedly had little success implementing the performance consulting skills on the job. Upon meeting with the group that was able to learn with the aid of webcams six months later, all participants were able to report success stories using their new performance consulting skills.

From this experience I've concluded that the skills required in performance consulting—learning to read people and interpret communication—may very well rely on being able to at least see the individual in order for complete communication to take place. I believe this holds true for both the role-play behavior and the group feedback process. This one experience does not provide enough data to definitively say that social presence is necessary to achieve skill building in a virtual classroom, but it made a believer out of me.

What research there is on social presence goes on to say that not enough instructional designers take social presence into account when designing virtual classroom experiences. Social presence may not be as necessary for information presentation; however, for a skill-building instructional strategy, social presence can be a powerful tool.

REVIEWING AND REVISING DELIVERABLES

Reviewing and making revisions to Participant's and Facilitator's Guides is difficult work that requires laserlike attention to detail. If the techniques you used in other phases of the Handshaw model—reviewing analysis and design documents, gaining consensus in the blueprint meeting, validating the prototype with sample learners—were successful, then this part of the process should be worry free.

It is especially important for you to give your reviewers a schedule prior to sending out detailed design documents such as Facilitator's Guides and Participant's Guides for review. Based on the length of the document, you need to give your reviewers as much time as you can for a detailed review. You also have to remember that reviewing your documents is probably an additional task for your reviewers and not part of their normal work. Creating a schedule for all your reviews, with dates for delivery of the documents and signoff with recommended revisions, is a good practice and should be done at the beginning of the project, if you can be that organized. If you can't commit to a complete schedule at the beginning of the project, at least give your reviewers a week or two of notice about when they will have to review the level of detail required for your Participant's and Facilitator's Guides. You can also save some time by letting each of your reviewers know that you are looking for completeness and accuracy and that you need them to correct errors on the copy whenever possible.

The process will undoubtedly reveal differing opinions on the content, so act quickly to resolve these issues. Ideally, these differences of opinion would have been caught during the task analysis phase, but it's better to discover such problems now rather than later, when the training is delivered.

CONTINUING THE PRODUCTION PHASE . . .

Chapter 9 continues in the Production phase of the Handshaw Instructional Design Model. If you develop a lot of e-learning programs, Chapter 9 helps you get better results from these programs. For strategies in which instructor-led training is needed to build skills, e-learning, done well, can provide the knowledge that is a prerequisite for the skill-building classes. The most common type of blended learning solutions used today are a combination of e-learning for knowledge and instructor-led training for skill building.

Designing for E-Learning

This chapter continues the focus on the Production phase of the model (Figure 9.1), but concentrates specifically on e-learning. The term *e-learning* as used in this book refers to self-paced learning delivered via a computer (desktop or laptop).

Telling—no matter how easily understood or well packaged the information being told—is not the same as training. Harold D. Stolovitch and his wife, Erica J. Keeps, have made "Telling Ain't Training" a catchphrase in the training and development community through their bestselling book of the same name, *Telling Ain't Training,* and a series of nationwide workshops. Their work forms the basis for what I call the "teachable moment" in e-learning.

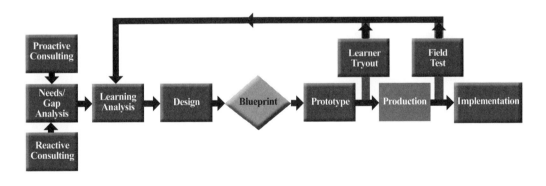

FIGURE 9.1   Handshaw Instructional Design Model: Production

THE "TEACHABLE MOMENT" IN E-LEARNING

If you ask e-learning developers whether their learners actually read or listen to all the information they include in their courses, the answer is almost always "no." People learn through practice and feedback. The teachable moment in e-learning comes from that magic moment when a learner makes a mistake in a simulation, or picks the wrong answer to a challenging question, and is presented with a hint or feedback. When this happens, learners stop everything and pay attention. I have observed this many times as I conduct learner tryouts. Learners light up with that "Aha!" realization and become truly engaged. How you manage this moment of attention and interest is the most important part of your e-learning course.

Create teachable moments by giving your learners the opportunity to do something that requires feedback. Make the most of the teachable moments by providing an opportunity for learners to try again, perhaps offering a hint or supplying some new knowledge that might enable those learners to succeed.

▶ Designing Opportunities to Interact

E-learning designers are always looking for ways to create interaction in their e-learning programs. Creating theme games, like *Jeopardy,* may be interesting, but many learners find that these games slow them down and get in the way of their learning. Some clients ask to have the game portions of e-learning courses removed after a few months, as a result of complaints from their learners.

If you've been writing performance objectives and designing your measurement and instructional strategies from those objectives, you won't need to invent interaction opportunities. Sometimes a gaming approach is great, especially if it really simulates what is required on the job. Simulations and simulation games are effective if they are used in context. As my friend Tony

O'Driscoll points out, "Content may be king, but context is the kingdom." For content to be effective it must be put in the context of the actual job. Using joblike simulations is a great strategy if it's supported by decision points or targeted questions. Practice and feedback provide that teachable moment and the basis for confidence building on the job.

▶ Sample Strategies for E-Learning

I have defined the teachable moment as the point at which the learner has been asked to do something or answer a question and has failed or possibly succeeded by making a guess. It is at this point that we have the individual's attention, and it is what we do next that helps that person discover and learn.

Here are just a few of the possible strategies that you can apply to the requirements of your performance objectives. Make sure they match up with the action portion of your objective and then just add a little creativity.

- **Software simulation:** Teaching employees to use new software systems is a successful and popular strategy used in e-learning. Teaching users to apply the new software to actually do their jobs should go way beyond where to click and what to key in a field. The focus needs to be on the job, not just the system. If the learner must interact with a customer in completing the job, include that customer interaction in the simulation. If you did your task analysis properly, it will serve as a road map for completing this type of software simulation and will help you include instruction for the complete task.

- **Task simulation:** E-learning is an excellent way for learners to acquire operational practice. The goal is to allow the learner to identify components and even operate machinery in a graphically simulated environment before operating the real thing. Practicing with the real thing may eventually have to be done with an instructor or coach. This practice takes less time and is more successful if feedback can be provided in a simulated environment ahead of time.

- **Simulation game:** Simulations with scoring components can help keep learners engaged if they are used appropriately. In the previous simulation examples, you might design a game that scores players based on how many correct system choices are made. Review the audience and learning culture analyses to find the preference and culture clues needed to make the right decision about when to use a simulation game.

- **Structured role play:** Sometimes it's not practical to bring learners together for a classroom experience even though doing so is the best design decision. You can be creative by simulating the role play with e-learning. For example, an e-learning program might include a video of an actor beginning a sales or service scenario with a customer. Learners respond to a series of questions about this scenario and are prompted to choose the most appropriate action. Feedback is provided with a realistic reaction from the customer. For instance, a wrong choice in a customer service scenario could branch to a video of the customer's negative reaction. This form of feedback puts the customer response in the context of the actual job and often makes for an unforgettable learning experience.

- **Tutorial:** The tutorial strategy is effective for objectives that require presentation of information. This strategy consists of presenting information through text, graphics, animation, or pictures with embedded objective-type test questions to check for comprehension. This strategy may not be exciting, but it works better than a PowerPoint presentation with a sound track and no interaction or practice at all. Be careful to select a question type that measures the level of learned capability required by the performance objective. Remember to refer to Figure 5.2 for a handy job aid to help you select the best type of objective question.

- **Drill and practice:** In a world where we can easily look things up or where we can provide performance support tools, we don't need to rely on memory as much as we used to. But there are still some situations where quick recall is required. For performance objectives that require recall of information, providing drill and practice with or without a gaming or scoring component can be a successful strategy. Just be sure you select this strategy for the right reasons.

There is one thing all these strategies have in common. They all provide for practice and feedback. It takes more time to use these strategies correctly, but they all take advantage of the teachable moment.

WRITING PRESCRIPTIVE FEEDBACK

The teachable moment works only when your learner makes a mistake answering a question or selects a wrong choice in a simulation. You can visibly observe this in a learner tryout when you see your learner slow down and focus attention on the e-learning. What happens next determines whether your learner progresses or falls back into passive reading mode.

Feedback, more than any other aspect of e-learning, can make for successful e-learning experiences. For feedback to be effective, I recommend that you use what I call *prescriptive feedback*. The popular multiple-choice question can serve as a good example for how prescriptive feedback works. Suppose a learner selects a wrong answer to a multiple-choice question, and the only available feedback is that the answer is incorrect. The incorrect response is scored, and the learner continues the program without really knowing what was wrong with the answer. I have observed this exact scenario in learner try-outs. The result is that learners become discouraged, which causes them to disengage.

Suppose instead that your learner is provided with a well-written hint and an opportunity to try again. The real "Aha!" moment comes when the learner selects the correct answer based on the hint. In learner tryouts this is characterized by visible body language and, often, a positive comment. In any event, learner engagement increases. Even in the case where the learner guesses the correct answer but knows it was just a lucky guess, the correct answer feedback should include information telling the learner why the answer is correct. Having the learner select the correct answer is not important. It is the feedback that provides the teachable moment. If your learner gets an incorrect answer on the second try, the e-learning should provide a feedback message revealing the correct answer with an explanation of why that answer is correct. The best way for you to judge how well your feedback is working is to observe your learners in a learner tryout.

▶ Prescriptive Feedback Suggestions

You can apply prescriptive feedback to any of the instructional strategies covered in this chapter. Here are some suggestions to help you create your own e-learning prescriptive feedback responses:

- **Correct answer feedback:** Sometimes a learner guesses the correct answer and still does not understand why it is correct. Always provide the reason that a particular answer is correct.

- **First wrong answer feedback:** Don't give the answer away after the learner's first incorrect response. Provide a hint that stimulates a higher level of thinking. It is rewarding in a learner tryout to watch a learner deduce a correct answer from your well-written feedback. Learners become more engaged every time this happens.

■ **Second wrong answer feedback:** If the learner does not get the answer on the second try, it is unlikely that any further hint will help, so reveal the correct answer. Let the learner know that the response was incorrect. Reveal the correct response, and explain why it is correct.

■ **Catchall feedback:** This type of feedback is used frequently in simulations. There are so many actions a learner could take in a system simulation, and you can't anticipate all of them. You must provide instructions to direct the learner to the desired action.

With all these suggestions, it is up to you, the designer, how many tries you want to allow your learners. Providing one additional try is usually enough before providing the correct answer. You can easily determine how many tries work best by observing your design in a learner tryout. Why guess when you can measure—right?

▶ The Power of Prescriptive Feedback

Prescriptive feedback isn't new, but e-learning is often designed without it. It does take more time to include these feedback responses, but it is ultimately worth it. Pay attention during the learner tryout, and you'll have a good idea of how many tries and what kind of feedback are needed. If you are concerned about how long it takes to write prescriptive feedback, consider that it may take less time to write good feedback than it does to write too much content, which your learners won't read anyway.

Keep your content presentation brief, and rely mainly on interactive strategies, practice, and feedback to provide the learning. An acceptable strategy might be to present simple concepts with a question or a simulation exercise and then allow the feedback to provide the instruction. Correct responses on the first try allow learners to read more or move on. Incorrect answers on the first try allow learners to learn on their own and be coached to the right answer. In either case, you can be sure that you've engaged the learners.

This approach makes e-learning self-paced and personalized, which are benefits of this type of learning. There are times when you have to produce quick informational programs with little opportunity for interaction. But when you are designing something that requires learners to be able to perform important tasks and use knowledge to solve problems, prescriptive feedback used during the teachable moment is the most efficient and effective way to get the job done.

▶ What Learners Need from E-Learning

Beyond providing teachable moments for your learners, there are some simple things that just make it easier for them to get what they need from e-learning. Here are some tips for keeping your courses useful and relevant:

- **Consistent, obvious navigation:** Design the user interface to be intuitive and straightforward. Keep it simple by not including features your learners won't use. Avoid the temptation to use too many cool or cute features. The user interface is not a place to be overly creative. Simplicity and economy are what learners need here.

- **Personalized instruction:** No one likes being trained on something they already know—or think they know. E-learning doesn't have to be linear, unless the audience and task analyses indicate that all the learners have the same skill level. If your analyses tell you that your audience has different levels of expertise regarding your topic, e-learning is a great tool for customizing or personalizing the instruction to fit individual needs. You can offer a pretest so learners can test out of certain learning objectives. You can offer a customized menu approach, or you can require all learners to take all modules in sequence.

- **Lean content:** It is especially important to keep e-learning content lean. Try presenting concepts in the form of discovery questions instead of using too much detail followed by embedded questions. Put more of your content into your feedback, and let the teachable moment do the work for you. If learners are successful during the learner tryout, you are not leaving out important content. It is better to start out lean and add more content later if you discover you need to.

- **Clear, conversational tone:** This advice goes hand in hand with the previous bullet point. Write feedback and other comments directed to the learners in clear, easy-to-understand language. Imagine that you're talking directly to the learner, and record that conversation or comment. In most cases, this language will be clear and concise.

- **Context for the Job Task:** Learners often question the relevance of content and how it applies to their jobs. You must constantly relate your content to the job task in order to meet the needs of learners. If you can't decide whether certain content is relevant to the job task, review the task analysis to check for fit and then make your decision.

- **Graphics:** An overabundance of graphics in e-learning design is just decoration, or what I call "gratuitous graphics." An interesting and appealing look is desirable, but it is important to know how the look and feel of your course supports the ultimate goal of learning. If you're unsure about what kind of graphics to use, consult the learning culture analysis. You should also evaluate the relevance of your graphics during a learner tryout. Award-winning, cool-looking e-learning courses are fine, but the job of an instructional designer is to deliver business results.

■ **Audio:** Audio serves a purpose when it is an integral part of a demonstration, such as a role play, or for audiences with documented low reading levels. Sounds may serve as signals or stimuli in a manufacturing process. Forcing a learner to listen to one thing while trying to read another is distracting. Always use audio with purpose in mind, not just because it's an option. Audio can also add unnecessary expense when updating or doing other maintenance work on an e-learning course.

■ **Performance-appropriate measurement:** E-learning measurement, as in any kind of training, must be appropriate for the required performance. The best guide for making this decision is the capability verb and the action portion of the performance objectives. Once again, you can use the table in Figure 5.2 to help you choose the capability verb to identify what type of testing instrument is appropriate for a given level of learned capability.

➧ Writing Better Test Questions

Writing test questions is part of the production process. Figure 9.2 is a guide that my staff has developed over several years to help you write better e-learning questions quickly and efficiently.

Guide for Writing Better Test Questions

True/False or Yes/No Questions

- Try to state the question positively.

- Express a single idea in each item.

- Express the statement as simply and as clearly as possible.

- Base the item on statements that are absolutely true or false, without qualifications or exceptions. (Avoid terms like: Never, Always, None, Usually, Sometimes, Frequently, Generally, etc.)

- False items tend to discriminate more highly than true items. Therefore, use more false items than true items (but no more than 15% additional false items).

- Avoid "lifting" the statement from text, lecture, or other materials.

- Include enough background information and qualifications so that the ability to respond correctly to the item does not depend on some special, uncommon knowledge.

Matching and Ranking Questions

- Use more options than items to reduce guessing by process of elimination.

- Always give directions since this question type is not one you will use often, and the directions can be complicated. Explain whether or not a response can be used more than once and indicate how and where to record the answer.

- Be sure all the items are in the same category, i.e., homogeneous.

- Arrange the list of responses in some systematic order, if possible (e.g., chronological, alphabetical).

- Keep the matching items brief, 10 or fewer.

- When possible, reduce reading time by using short phrases or single words.

- Maintain parallel grammatical structure for answer items.

Completion (Fill-in-the-Blank) Questions

- Omit only significant words from the statements.

- Do not omit so many words from the statement that the meaning is lost.

- Avoid grammatical or other clues to the correct response.

- Make the blanks of equal length.

- Try to put the blank at the end of the sentence, after the problem.

- Limit the desired response to a single word or very short phrase.

- Allow for misspellings whenever spelling accuracy is not required.

(continues)

Single-Select and Multiple-Select Questions

Stem:

- When possible, state the stem as a direct question rather than an incomplete statement.
- Present a definite, explicit, and singular question or problem.
- Avoid excess verbage.
- Include in the stem any word that might otherwise be repeated in the alternatives.
- Use negatively stated items sparingly. When used, underline and/or capitalize the negative.

Alternatives (choices):

- All options should be plausible. A humorous option here and there is OK.
- Make alternatives grammatically parallel and consistent with the stem.
- When possible, present alternatives in a logical order.
- Use at least 4 alternatives to lower the guessing probabilities.
- Randomly distribute the correct response(s) among alternative positions.
- Avoid using "none of the above" and "all of the above"; use a Multiple Select question instead.
- If using Single Select, make sure there is only one correct response.

Essay Questions

- Prepare the item to elicit the behavior you want to measure.
- Phrase the item so the learner's task is clearly indicated.
- Indicate a point value or estimated time for answering.
- Ask questions to elicit responses on which experts could agree that one answer is better than another.
- Avoid giving the student a choice among optional items, because this reduces the reliability of the test.

Performance Test

- Prepare items that elicit the behavior you want to measure.
- Clearly identify and explain the simulated situation.
- Make the simulated situations as realistic as possible.
- Provide clear directions.
- If "live", adequately train the observers/scorers to ensure that they are fair and consistent in scoring the appropriate behaviors.

FIGURE 9.2   Guide for Writing Better Test Questions

CONTINUING THE PRODUCTION PHASE . . .

The Production phase is such a time-consuming phase that it requires three full chapters to do it justice. Chapter 10 describes the Production phase for performance support and m-learning. Performance support is one of the most important and often ignored learning strategies. M-learning is also included in Chapter 10 because it's an increasingly popular way to distribute performance support and other learning support.

Designing for Performance Support and M-Learning

Performance support can be one of the most cost-effective choices for delivering training. Instructor-led training and e-learning (covered in Chapters 8 and 9) are the two most popular delivery systems for blended learning solutions. M-learning is a popular and effective choice for delivering learning or performance support to mobile devices for just-in-time learning and support. Both performance support and m-learning are developed during the Production phase of the Handshaw Instructional Design Model (see Figure 10.1).

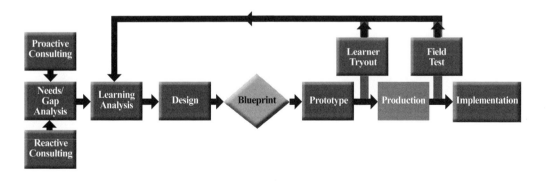

FIGURE 10.1 Handshaw Instructional Design Model: Production

PERFORMANCE SUPPORT ENSURES RESULTS

Performance support is your best investment with regard to a choice of learning delivery systems. You can debate whether it is really a training solution or "just" a support tool, as the name implies. The point is, the ability of many learners to transfer what they learned into actual practice on the job often depends on performance support. Best of all, performance support tools are relatively inexpensive to create and easy to deliver.

Since the publication of Gloria Gery's book *Electronic Performance Support Systems*, each new wave of technological innovation changed how performance support is designed and used. It's hardly surprising that mobile computing technology (m-learning) is rapidly gaining ground as both a learning and a performance support solution.

For many learners, performance support is an essential tool to help them transfer learning into actual on-the-job skills. Implementing a performance support solution can solve a problem without the need to develop training at all.

What follows are suggestions for how to incorporate a wide variety of performance support solutions into your design, ensuring learning transfer on the job and providing a business benefit to your client or organization.

▶ Paper Job Aids

Paper job aids provide a reference for anything that eventually goes into memory as a result of repetitive use (see Figure 10.2). Sometimes job aids provide a reference for information that never needs to go into memory. Job aids fall into two categories. In the first category, learners may discontinue use of the job aids once they are proficient at the job. The job aid may serve as a temporary crutch, needed only while learning a new task. In the second category, a more permanent job aid may be needed if it is to be used for things that are not done on a repetitive basis.

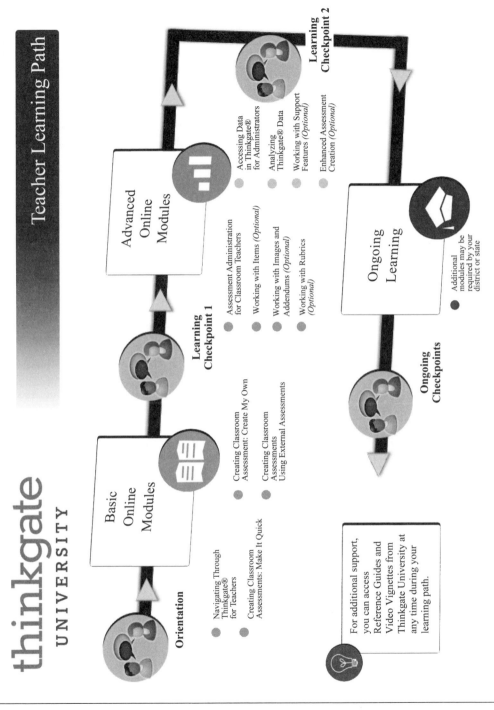

FIGURE 10.2 Sample Paper Job Aid

▶ Electronic Performance Support Systems (EPSSs)

An EPSS offers a more sophisticated range of options than a simple job aid, including audio and video interactivity and the option of hyperlinks to deliver more specific detail if needed. Even though electronic support is more expensive to develop and deliver than job aids, an EPSS can be a less expensive option than developing and delivering training. Electronic forms of performance support are usually indicated where more permanent solutions are needed, and they often accompany a training program. The use of EPSSs can become an important part of the job task or procedure. Performance support is often prescribed as part of a performance improvement initiative as a substitute for training.

M-LEARNING: THE NEXT LOGICAL PROGRESSION OF E-LEARNING

In order to better understand where trends are going, it's helpful to look at where they've been. The success and proliferation of e-learning have largely been a matter of access, as you can see in the following timeline.

▶ A Brief History of E-Learning

Mainframe, 1980s

- This was the first practical way to design and deliver training with the aid of a computer.

- Presentation was limited to text characters.

- Interactivity was an option if used creatively.

- Prescriptive feedback and answer judging were used.

- It included pretest and posttests with scoring.

- It was called computer-based training (CBT).

Stand-alone PC, late 1980s

- It used a 16-color display with the ability to display simple graphic images.

- It could develop and deliver courses anywhere without the need for connectivity.

- It had robust interactivity and answer-judging capabilities.

- The authoring efficiency was improved.

Local area networks (LANs), wide area networks (WANs), 1990s

- This used distributed computing, with PCs connected to servers, usually with access to mainframes.

- It used a 16-color display with the ability to display simple graphic images.

- It was a big step forward in terms of access.

- Companies could reach far more employees through LANs and eventually through WANs.

- It was easy to maintain and update courses for multiple learners.

Multimedia learning systems, early 1990s

■ This used more powerful PCs and delivered higher-resolution graphics, photos, video, and audio.

■ Storage was on large video discs, and later CDs and DVDs.

■ Interaction possibilities were exciting but time consuming and expensive to develop and distribute.

■ Many successful experimental programs were developed with these powerful new tools.

Internet—online learning, late 1990s

■ No longer called computer-based training; this was the new era of e-learning.

■ The possibilities for access increased dramatically.

■ It involved a trade-off in the area of bandwidth.

■ E-learning developers were temporarily ushered back to the dark ages of text only.

■ As bandwidth options improved, we had the best of both worlds, with rich media and easy access available to almost anyone with a computer and an Internet connection.

Mobile learning (m-learning), mid-2000s

■ This was the biggest leap forward yet in terms of access, with the proliferation of tablets and smart phones.

- Lots of rich media were available.

- One valuable asset of the computer was lost: screen size.

- It was time to adapt once again . . .

▶ Hurdles for M-Learning

There are always new and evolving development tools. In addition, there are incompatibilities among software platforms, Internet browsers, and multiple devices. These hurdles are not good reasons to avoid using new technologies—the hurdles always go away in good time. What doesn't go away is bad design. Do your best to deal with the hurdles and put your best efforts into good analysis and design.

Responsive Design is a software development technique that helps solve the problem of different screen sizes among mobile devices. The tool was originally designed to help websites provide an optimal viewing experience. Responsive Design techniques help you do the same thing with your m-learning solutions.

The challenges of m-learning are solvable. If your design process tells you that you have a perfect application for m-learning, do your homework with your delivery systems analysis, find good technical support, and jump in. Solving problems and creating something new and exciting can be rewarding to your clients and your career.

▶ Strategies for M-Learning

The decision to select m-learning as a possible solution goes back to the Design phase. Based on data from your performance objectives, audience analysis, learning culture analysis, and delivery systems analysis, you will be able to tell whether your needs match the unique capabilities of m-learning. A learning application is probably more suited to a tablet than to a smart phone. M-learning is also suitable as part of a blended solution, whereby smaller amounts of information can act as a reminder or as performance support. Following are some suggestions for strategies for using m-learning.

- **Performance support:** M-learning offers an endless list of options for performance support, from public- and private-sector regulation compliance to medical procedure applications and the documentation of maintenance procedures. We actually used m-learning to document the condition of damaged electric utility lines caused by bird droppings.

- **Measurement for performance tests:** When performance tests are used as measurement for a procedural task, the mobile device can be used by an evaluator to grade a checklist that is connected to a learning management system. The LMS can determine which learning objects were mastered successfully and prescribe remedial learning steps for those that were not mastered.

- **Just-in-time reminder:** This is similar to performance support, but it's even better. The difference is that reminders can be customized or at least configured to individual needs. Another important ingredient for this strategy is to make sure the reminder is just enough. If there is too much content, it won't work as a reminder.

- **Collaborative learning:** Learners can share text, photos, and video to give each other feedback or ask for help. There are times when even a phone call works best! Once the initial application is created, the collaborative learning program can take on a life of its own with very little additional investment. Check your learning culture analysis to make sure you can fit this type of learning into your current culture. You may have to prepare that culture ahead of time to make this strategy successful.

- **Individual coaching:** Individual coaching is effective but expensive, whether it's done in person or remotely. The video camera in your mobile device can be used to send examples both ways during coaching sessions. These just-in-time sessions can happen anywhere, anytime without requiring a face-to-face meeting. This makes coaching more cost effective, with easy access for learners.

THE NEXT PHASE . . .

With the Production phase behind you, it's time to validate your final product with a field test. No matter how carefully you have followed your process, there will be improvements you will want to make before you release them to your audience. It's time to ask your learners to help make your solution as good as it can be. The experience of observing your learners interact with the instructional materials will push you to be a better designer.

CHAPTER 11

Validating Success with a Field Test

O rganizing a field test is a final opportunity to ensure that your design performs to your learners' expectations. The field test takes place at the conclusion of the Production phase, when the entire learning solution is basically finished (see Figure 11.1). The field test actually becomes an extension of the Production phase. During the field test, you gather data to correct any deficiencies in the solution. Just as in the learner tryout, you should turn to the best possible source for this data—the people who have to learn from your solution.

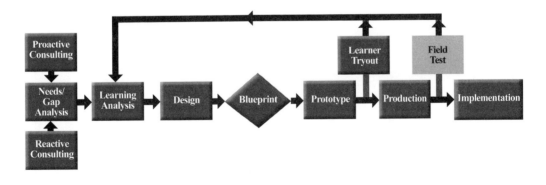

FIGURE 11.1   Handshaw Instructional Design Model: Field Test

PLANNING AND IMPLEMENTING THE FIELD TEST

The only additional time required to conduct a field test is the time to plan and implement the event. Using the cost-vs.-risk rule, weigh the risk that your solution might have a few flaws against the time it takes to plan and implement the event. In some cases you may not need to conduct a field test. This is a flexible model, and you only need to use the steps that are necessary or appropriate. If the learning solution supports an important, new enterprise-wide initiative, you probably want to know what is going to happen before it goes to the entire audience. Think of the field test as an insurance policy for your work. How much time is that worth?

The field test is similar to, but slightly different from, the learner tryout. In the learner tryout, you validate the measurement and instructional strategies exemplified by the prototype. The learner tryout helps you determine whether you need to make revisions to either of these high-level strategies before you continue with the time-consuming work in the Production phase. The field test helps you determine whether your completed solution works with the intended audience as it's supposed to. The field test helps you identify content descriptions that are unclear to your learners. You can also identify questions or performance tests that are difficult for learners to master. Finally, this is your last chance to find typos and other language errors.

▶ Planning

Planning for the field test is divided into three categories: audience selection and preparation, event logistics, and data gathering. All three are discussed in more detail as follows:

- **Audience selection and preparation:** Your client may want to add subject matter experts to the field test audience. In the event that you have SMEs in your audience, be aware that your reliable data will come from learners who actually represent your audience as described by your audience analysis. Having SMEs as part of the field test may help you find any additional errors of completeness and accuracy, but they will not indicate whether the learning solution enables your learners to achieve the intended results. The key participants are the sample learners described in your audience analysis. For a field test of instructor-led training, I recommend a minimum of twenty participants. The audience size for e-learning or a virtual classroom can be larger, but having at least twenty learners provides enough data to reveal trends or failures in the learning solution. If you have twenty sample learners, you won't need to select them as carefully as you did in the learner tryout. Taking a particular work group or any randomly selected group of twenty learners will suffice.

- **Event logistics:** This is your opportunity to test your implementation plan with a smaller audience that has been recruited to help you. The field test is your chance to make a good first impression with your training solution. You must pay attention to details in order to make sure that first implementation goes well. The development of your implementation plan is covered in Chapter 5. Chapter 12 discusses the actual implementation in greater detail.

- **Data gathering:** Collecting data from your field test is easy if you plan your efforts ahead of time. The field test audience should be larger than the learner tryout sample. You should conduct the test to simulate the actual learning environment as closely as possible. Unlike the learner tryout, the data collection in this test needs to be less of a distraction to users. Instead of observing each learner one-on-one, you should provide your sample learners with their own checklists to write down anything they like or dislike about the solution, including any questions or problems they might have. You can also conduct pre- and posttest interviews to document attitudes or opinions about the training or choice of delivery system.

▶ Good Results, Bad Results

Although you do want to make a good impression on your learning audience, the goal of a field test is not for everything to go perfectly. The goal is to collect data. Whether it's good news or bad news, data is helpful in terms of making any needed revisions to your training solution before you release it to your entire audience.

Some learning organizations resist conducting a field test because of the time it requires. The only extra time required is the time it takes to observe that first audience and review the data that you collect. One reason training organizations don't conduct field tests is that they are afraid of finding unanticipated results. In reality, you should be afraid of *not* finding problems before you release any training solution to an audience, large or small. The bad results simply tell you what needs to be changed or fixed before the course is released.

▶ Conducting the Field Test

The field test is a more formal experience than the informal and open-ended learner tryout. The goal is to simulate the learning environment as closely as possible. If you have decided to change your learning environment in any way, you need to inform your learners of the intended change and make sure they understand the benefits of that change.

In the field test, you are training your first group of learners while you ask them to collect data for you. Data collection is not necessarily secondary, but it should be done so that it does not interfere with the actual learning. Here is how the test is conducted:

1. **Introduce the field test:** Explain the valuable role your learners will play in the final validation and quality control for the training program, just as you did in the learner tryout. Encourage their input, and be sure you collect all comments. Don't discuss the comments or make any decisions on them during the test. Don't be discouraged if some learners write down very few comments. Others will provide more than enough feedback.

2. **Collect data:** Provide each learner with a checklist, and give everyone instructions on how to complete them. Observers are in charge of distributing and collecting checklists from everyone. Use subject matter experts as coaches. Caution the coaches to allow the instruction to fail first if there is a problem. The failure allows the observers to identify a problem. The coaches can step in to help the learner solve the problem in order to continue.

3. **Conduct pre- and posttest interviews:** Pre and posttest interviews may reveal attitudes or other useful information. You should keep these interviews short. Asking five questions should take twenty minutes or so. These questions will serve you best if they are asked by the observers and written down by them rather than the learner. This type of personal interview also gives you the chance to ask further probing questions when an interesting point is brought to light by the learner. It is important to keep an open mind to whatever type of new information you might find.

➧ Analyzing Results and Making Revisions

The data from a field test is used primarily by the instructional design team to make final revisions and remove any surprises before releasing the program to the entire target audience. It is a quality assurance step that doesn't have to

Observer Notes

Commercial Lending Training

Name:	*Sample Learner*

Introduction to Commercial Lending

Comfort Level Key:

1. Very Comfortable — No hesitation, works with confidence.

2. Comfortable — Slight hesitation, but no confusion.

3. Neutral — Significant hesitation, somewhat confused—but no problems.

4. Uncomfortable — Confused, problems arise that temporarily stop work but are quickly resolved.

Start: *9:42*

Finish: *10:00*

5. Very Uncomfortable — Very confused, serious problems arise that stop work until external intervention is provided.

Comfort with Interactions		
Element	**Comfort**	**Comments**
Navigation	*1*	*Very easy to use for a non-tech-savvy person*
Conceptual information	*1*	*On the screen that points out the parenthesis, point to an example*
Guided practice	*1.5*	• *Tried to type and then click the next button, instead of pressing Tab (from 13 of 20 learners)* • *Missed the directions to press Tab after a text entry and got stuck (from 10 of 20 learners)* • *No problems with practice* • *Preferred Enter over Tab* • *Tried to click the Add Line button instead of the forward arrow (from 12 of 20 learners)* • *Would like to search by relationship or group instead of customer*

FIGURE 11.2 Completed Checklists and Compiled Data *(Note: See the compilation of how many learners made the same comment in parentheses. These indicate significant trends to consider for revisions.)*

be shared with clients and stakeholders before repairs are made. Figure 11.2 shows a single completed checklist and a tally of compiled data from checklists. Note how the data conclusively points out some necessary revisions.

THE NEXT PHASE . . .

The Implementation phase, discussed in Chapter 12, is the last stage of the model. This phase consists of implementing your design according to your plan, gathering measurement data, evaluating the data, and, finally, proving the business impact of your design and in some cases measuring the return on investment (ROI) in learning.

Implementation:
The Final Guarantee
of Results

Most instructional design models include logistical steps for implementing instruction but don't go any further. In an instructional design model that delivers results, the Implementation phase has to go further than just implementing training. The Implementation phase has to measure and can even guarantee the expected results. (See Figure 12.1.)

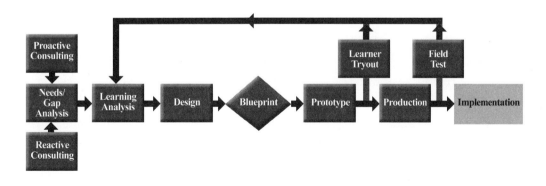

FIGURE 12.1 Handshaw Instructional Design Model: Implementation

IMPLEMENTING YOUR PLAN

Developing a well-designed training program and a detailed implementation plan does not guarantee business results. Using the implementation plan you created during the Design phase (see Chapter 5) is only part of the implementation process. However, using the implementation plan isn't a 100 percent guarantee of results. To make my point, I have included two examples of plans, both of which were good plans. One led to success, and the other had mixed results.

▶ Fully Executed Implementation Plan

Our team was contracted to design a new store manager training program for a client that was preparing for an initial public offering (IPO). Wall Street analysts predicted that our client would not be able to maintain quality while growing the company. The store manager position was key to maintaining quality. This in turn made the store manager training program an important strategy in the IPO initiative. The current training solution was not scalable, nor was it truly measurable or consistent in its results. All store managers were being trained in a four-week classroom course on the East Coast. New store franchise owners on the West Coast were required to send their store managers east for a month of training before they could open their franchise.

The company's business goal for the IPO was to scale growth while maintaining the high-quality product and service that the company was known for. The training plan was to cut class time by 50 percent while establishing a consistent standard for performance measurement.

The solution was an e-learning front end that presented knowledge components of service, cleanliness, operations, and finance for store managers. All actual hands-on skills were done in the remaining two weeks of class time, and consistent performance tests were graded with the use of a checklist.

The implementation plan required all learners to complete the e-learning with a minimum score of 90 percent before attending the two-week hands-on class. Failure to successfully complete the e-learning would make it difficult or impossible for learners to succeed in the class. Worse yet, those individuals would delay the progress of the entire class if they couldn't keep up or required more of the instructor's time. The new two-week schedule would not allow for delays.

The success of the plan relied on management's commitment to require learners to successfully complete the e-learning before attending the class. The instructor had to deny only one student access to the class based on his failure to complete the e-learning. Once word got out, everyone else completed the e-learning with a passing score and on time. The training solution and implementation were so effective, the instructor said that he could turn out "a better prepared store manager in a two-week classroom experience than he could in the four-week program without the e-learning course."

The company and franchise owners were pleased with the results of the training program, which provided qualified store managers in less time. The IPO was completed, and the stock price rose well ahead of predictions.

▶ Partially Executed Implementation Plan

In another example, our client used a similar blended strategy of an e-learning course before a hands-on class. This client achieved successful results from their training and the implementation plan for a year or so. During a routine client visit two years after the initial implementation, our senior instructional designer was invited to observe a class from this earlier successful training program.

The class that our designer attended included five participants. Two had taken the prerequisite web-based training, and three had not. Our designer asked the two who took the training for their opinions of the course. They liked the system-simulated, hands-on practice in the e-learning portion. They told our designer that after completing the practice, the mastery test was easy to complete with a high score. During class, these two participants emerged as the successful performers—they were the first to finish, answered many of the instructor's questions, and even assisted the other learners. The other three learners struggled during the class and had a frustrating and unsatisfactory experience.

The results show that our client was successful when the initial implementation plan was carefully followed at the completion of the course. Over time, the implementation plan was no longer enforced, and the results suffered accordingly.

▶ The Influence of Culture on Implementation

In my experience, I have seen more good training solutions fail due to poor implementation than because of any other single factor. The reason for this failure can be summed up in one word: culture. In the two case studies cited previously, the only difference between them was a strong and deliberate culture versus a culture that lacked accountability. Both organizations were following a tested and successful instructional and measurement strategy, both followed similar implementation plans, but only one experienced success when the implementation plan was followed and fully executed.

Consult your learning culture analysis, and refer to it as you design and use your implementation plan. As you can see from our experience, just having an implementation plan doesn't guarantee results. Our experience at Handshaw has taught us that the closer we are to stakeholders and the true client, the more likely we are able to successfully help our client.

The relationships and the consensus that you built during your performance consulting and the blueprint meeting go a long way toward giving you the influence to follow through with the decisions outlined in your implementation plan. Too often, training organizations are prepared to declare victory and move on to the next project once a project is finished and ready for implementation. If you are truly committed to focusing on results rather than activities, you should take the time to sit down with your client and your team to review the implementation plan. This is also the time to revisit the business impact and ROI plan, if this is one of the projects you have selected for an ROI study.

MEASURING AND EVALUATING RESULTS

ROI and training evaluation gurus Jack and Patti Phillips often say in their presentations that since "you can't measure everything, you should decide what you can measure and just do that." It's a true statement about evaluation and many other activities or projects we all do. The bottom line is that you have to start somewhere.

By way of review from Chapter 5, *measurement* is the act of observing something and scoring the results according to a predetermined scale. Scoring learner mastery of performance objectives with a written or performance test is an example of measurement. *Evaluation,* on the other hand, is using measurement to apply value or judgment based on the measured results. Learner feedback on the value of instruction in helping them perform their jobs is an example of evaluation. It helps to be precise about the differences between these two terms as we proceed with this chapter.

⮞ Five Levels of Measurement and Evaluation

In their ROI Institute, Jack and Patti Phillips define five levels of measurement and evaluation. Applying these levels helps you implement your measurement strategy, which was determined during the Design phase.

1. **Reaction:** "Measures reaction to, and satisfaction with, the experience, contents, and value of the program." Almost

all training departments currently measure reaction to their training programs. Unfortunately, the results of level 1 evaluation are easily misinterpreted. High satisfaction with a learning experience does not always correlate with success in level 2, which measures what was actually learned or accomplished. For example, participants might not like their training experience because the instructor was uncompromising and pushed learners to succeed. On the other hand, a more likeable, less rigorous instructor might get high level 1 evaluation scores but produce fewer students who master the performance objectives. As you collect and evaluate data in Level 1, you should focus on the relevance of the content and the perceived value your learners place on how well the training helps them accomplish their job tasks.

2. **Learning:** "Measures what participants learned in the program—information, knowledge, skills, and contacts (take-aways from the program)." Learning is addressed primarily by the measurement strategy that you developed in the design phase. This is the level in which you use objective-type tests and performance tests to measure the degree of mastery that is achieved as a result of the program. Your data should strive to show the degree of mastery of the performance objectives. Research shows that less than half of all learning programs are subjected to a level 2 measurement.

3. **Application:** "Measures progress after the program—the use of information, knowledge, skills, and contacts." According to ROI Institute data, only 10 percent of training programs are measured at this level. It may not be practical to measure every participant if you have a large audience, but by surveying some

learners and managers you should have a good idea of how many behaviors from the program are actually being applied on the job. There is reliable data to suggest that managers have the greatest influence in encouraging the transfer of skills from training to on-the-job performance. As a by-product of measuring the level of application, you can accomplish more than just measuring results. Asking managers to measure the skills transfer from learning might encourage those managers to support the skills transfer.

4. **Business impact:** "Measures changes in business impact variables such as output, quality, time, and cost linked to the program." This level is applied to only 5 percent of all training programs. If you use the first three steps in the Handshaw model in a particular program, you should have your training goals aligned with business goals. Identifying and aligning the business goals to training goals makes measurement of business impact a lot easier.

5. **Return on investment:** "Compares the monetary benefits of the business impact to the costs of the program." According to the ROI Institute, you should target at least 5 percent of your training programs for calculating a return on investment. Targeting a small percentage of your training programs for calculating ROI does not place a huge burden of time and cost on your already stretched resources, but it can pay big dividends in information. Of course, you should target some of your best programs for measuring ROI. This shows the value and efficiency of the work that you and your team are doing. However, don't select only your best programs for measuring ROI. It can be equally valuable to target a program that didn't support an important business initiative. Selecting projects that you suspect

show a negative ROI helps clients and stakeholders appreciate the value of collecting data before making decisions about selecting and developing training in the future.

▶ Postimplementation Follow-Through

The measurement strategy that you designed during the Design phase and gained consensus for during the Blueprint phase allows you to complete evaluation and measurement levels 1 and 2. The information you gather here provides insight into how learners value the instruction and the impact on their daily job performance. The exercise also provides insight into the learner's mastery of your performance objectives. Levels 3 through 5, which deal with application, business impact, and ROI must be done postimplementation.

▶ Program Maintenance

Some organizations invest heavily in enterprise-wide, major training initiatives and never budget any time or money to maintain these initiatives. Regardless of the nature of the new initiative—a new software system, a new product launch, or a new or reengineered process—things change!

Projects large or small run the risk of falling into disuse and diminishing returns far ahead of their time if you haven't planned for ongoing maintenance. Savvy clients budget between 5 and 10 percent per year for maintenance of major initiatives that need to have a long shelf life. The design and development of training initiatives, especially those that are self-paced, must be seen as capital investments. Once they are developed and implemented, the return on investment only gets bigger year after year. This is why developing a culture of using data to evaluate your ROI can pay big dividends. The clients that do invest in maintenance programs increase the shelf life of their programs and see dramatic increases in their ROI.

THE NEXT CHALLENGE . . .

You have covered all phases of the Handshaw Instructional Design Model. Chapter 13 helps you implement the model in your organization and make it a sustainable part of your ongoing success.

Making Results Sustainable

This may well be the most important chapter in this book. Everything presented in the preceding pages is the result of many years of trial and error, experience, and continuous improvement on the part of myself and my staff. These practices are not difficult or time consuming. They all save time if they are used for the right reason in the right situations. The challenge now is for you to make these practices sustainable in your organization and in your work every day. You will only be able to achieve consistent business results with a model and practices that are sustainable. (See Figure 13.1.)

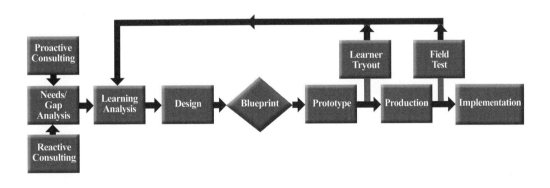

FIGURE 13.1   Handshaw Instructional Design Model

CHANGING YOUR ORGANIZATION'S FOCUS

Many learning organizations focus on the level of training activity because activity data is so readily available. Statistics for activity are far easier to come by than statistics to support results. Learning management systems provide companies with detailed reports to show how many learners spent how many hours in various learning activities. Data based on learning activities has become the most common source of information on training and is used by many executives to assess the value of their corporate training initiatives. Changing an organization's focus from activities to results can be a significant change management challenge.

▶ Focus on Results over Activities

In a business environment in which you are continually asked to do more with less, the Handshaw Instructional Design Model presents an opportunity to save time and resources while producing improved business results. Given the cost of both taking and developing training, corporations should be motivated to eliminate training that is unnecessary, of poor quality, or redundant. When training is developed, it must be focused on achieving the performance that brings about the desired business results. In order to get those results, business must move toward performance consulting and better training. The idea of doing more with less leads us in the wrong direction. As training professionals, we need to do less, and we need to do it better.

SUSTAINING YOUR CHANGE IN FOCUS

Adopting the best practices in the Handshaw Instructional Design Model requires a change management initiative that takes deliberate actions and time to complete. Once you assimilate these practices into your organization, you must have a plan to make the change sustainable. The following eight steps give you a plan to implement and sustain the Handshaw Instructional Design Model in your organization:

1. **Develop sponsorship, vision, and leadership:** The path to sustainability is to seek sponsorship and create a shared vision for how things will be done as the new design process is introduced and adopted. Define the process you are planning for and how it differs from the process you use today. This becomes the vision that you will use to gain sponsorship and inspire leaders throughout the sustainability process.

2. **Develop skills:** The goal is to begin working as a team so that you present a consistent methodology to your clients. Even if your team has good instructional design skills, the challenge may be in learning to work together in a consistent manner. Books and workshops are a good way to begin your skill development. Look inside and outside your organization for resources to help with this task.

3. **Identify agreed-upon best practices:** You and your team will interpret the model in this book in different ways. It is intended to be flexible and customized to your needs and your organization. The next step in changing your design process is to meet together as a team over a period of time to agree upon and document your best practices.

4. **Identify true clients within your client base:** Your team should meet to identify the true client within each department and discuss that client's individual needs. Some clients are more willing to try new things than others. You should begin your efforts with the clients that are easy to partner with.

Documenting successes with willing clients is the best path toward building a sustainable change.

5. **Develop relationships:** Once you have identified the most willing clients, position yourself as a trusted partner by applying the eight principles of proactive performance consulting from Chapter 2. After applying either proactive or reactive performance consulting skills, position yourself to complete a Gaps Map. You will be surprised at how the relationship changes once you begin asking about business goals and using the Gaps Map with your client. This changes the nature of the relationship and positions you as a strategic business partner.

6. **Manage change, timeline, and adoption:** As you begin using a new process with your clients, you must manage the change initiative. The use of the model itself and the blueprint meeting helps to manage expectations. Depending on your culture, you have to be careful how you manage the rate of change. Instead of implementing the whole model at once, your team may decide to phase in a few steps at a time. Develop a timeline for implementing the new process with your clients. The timeline should be measured in months or even years rather than weeks. Adoption of the entire process is gradual and rewarding.

7. **Develop solutions:** Be methodical and organized as you develop solutions, and use your new best practices as consistently as possible across your entire team.

8. **Measure success:** There is no better way to sustain any change initiative than measuring results and showcasing your success. A good example wins clients over to a new way of doing things better than explanations and promises. The model itself provides

many opportunities to plan, test the results, and provide measurable outcomes.

"BE THE CHANGE . . ."

You may not always have a team of colleagues to help you change to a new way of doing things, but you can be a one-person change initiative. One of my favorite quotes, often attributed to Gandhi, says "Be the change you wish to see in the world." Set your own goals and incremental measurements of success. Select just the right client to begin your change process. You may remember how important this was in my story of Bill, my first client (from Chapter 1).

In all my experience in this business, I have found that good clients who are willing to partner with you and share the risk of change are the best assurance of success. Sharing success with your client helps you sustain your new process.

CHAPTER 14

Conclusion

SUMMARY

The model in Figure 14.1 provides you with a systematic approach to designing instruction, which all instructional design models do. This one, however, focuses the instructional design team and client on results rather than activities. The model is intended to be flexible. You might never use it in its entirety, and you might never use it in the same way twice. It helps you focus your efforts on measurable results, whether the project is a short, temporary solution or an enterprise-wide major change initiative. As you practice using the model, your efforts will become easier and your results will become more successful.

> **Proactive performance consulting:** Initiate a series of regular meetings with your clients to inquire about the nature of the business and identify business goals. This positions you as a trusted business partner.

> **Reactive performance consulting:** Respond to training requests by linking the training request to a business goal and asking probing questions about the desired outcomes. This helps you

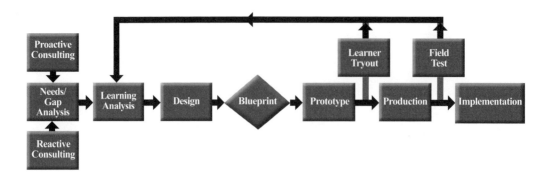

FIGURE 14.1   Handshaw Instructional Design Model

reframe the request to possibly eliminate the need for training, align the training to deliver business results, and/or identify other solutions in addition to training.

Needs/gap analysis: Meet with your true client to identify gaps in the business and performance outcomes by asking *should, is, cause* questions. Identify any causal links and formulate possible solutions to achieve the stated business goal. Include both training and nontraining solutions.

Analysis of training: If training is identified as a possible solution to a performance and business goal, analyze the task, audience, culture, and delivery systems as needed. You may be able to reuse prior analysis documents except in the case of the task analysis. A current task analysis must be completed with each new project in order for you and your client to agree upon the required performance outcomes.

Design: Write performance objectives to help your client and your entire project team further define performance outcomes and how to measure them. Use objectives to define a measurement and an instructional strategy. Design your implementation plan, including possible plans for measuring business impact and ROI.

Blueprint meeting: Gain consensus by presenting your recommendations for measurement and instructional strategies to your entire project team and provide opportunities for structured feedback. Make agreed-upon revisions to appropriate analysis and design documents.

Prototype: Develop a prototype that represents the measurement and instructional strategies that you and your team agreed upon during the blueprint meeting.

Learner tryout: Enlist sample learners to test your prototype in a controlled and structured learner tryout. Record feedback, and determine necessary revisions to your prototype and your overall measurement and instructional strategies.

Production: Using your analysis and design documents and a detailed content outline, produce all the required instructional and measurement instruments for your solution.

Field test: Enlist a group of sample learners to test your complete solution in a controlled and structured field test. Record feedback, and determine necessary revisions to your final solution.

Implementation: Implement your training solution according to your prepared implementation plan. Conduct any preplanned measurement of business impact and return on investment.

Sustainability: Apply your measurement to determine results. Successes help you sustain the momentum of using your new design practices. Failures help you refine your process or identify the need for more rigorous reframing and alignment with business goals.

A CALL TO ACTION

Taking responsibility for delivering results is quite different from doing what your clients ask you to do. You are taking a risk when you begin to ask about business goals and sharing the responsibility of achieving that goal with your client. The risk also has its rewards. The value of your individual contribution to your organization increases dramatically.

You will become a trusted and valued partner to your clients. You will become a leader and a role model to your colleagues. Find trusted advisers, believe in yourself, and help take our profession to a higher level.

Glossary

Action: In performance objectives, the description of "how" the learner will perform the task.

ADDIE: A generic form of instructional design models, which stands for Analyze, Design, Develop, Implement, Evaluate.

Application: The third level of the ROI Institute's five levels of measurement and evaluation, which "measures progress after the program—the use of information, knowledge, skills, and contacts," as defined by the ROI Institute.

Audience analysis: Describes the intended audience for a learning event in terms of general characteristics (demographics) and entry behaviors (what the audience already knows about the subject being taught).

Blueprint phase: A phase in the Handshaw Instructional Design Model in which the team reaches consensus about a solution by presenting recommendations for measurement and instructional strategies and implementation to the entire project team and provides opportunities for structured feedback.

Business impact: The fourth level of the ROI Institute's five levels of measurement and evaluation, which "measures changes in business impact variables such as output, quality, time, and cost linked to the program," as defined by the ROI Institute.

Business need: Describes the stated goal of a business initiative in strategic and measurable outcomes. These goals usually address money, accomplishments, or profitability.

Capability and work environment need: Describes whether the workforce has the skills, knowledge, and attributes required to succeed at the performance goal.

Cluster task analysis: A type of task analysis that is used when you come across content that must be categorized or processed so that the content can be applied to perform a specific task.

Combination task analysis: A type of task analysis that is used to depict the flow of both procedural and hierarchical tasks.

Computer-based training (CBT): An outdated term for e-learning. It was popular when e-learning was delivered on mainframe computer systems or on stand-alone or networked PCs.

Cost-vs.-risk rule: A tool that helps you determine which steps in the Handshaw Instructional Design Model should be used in a given situation and what resources should be spent on them.

Criterion-referenced tests (CRTs): Tests included in learning programs in which the performance or learning objectives become the criteria for measuring learner mastery.

Delivery systems analysis: A step in the Learning Analysis phase of the Handshaw Instructional Design Model in which existing learning delivery systems are analyzed for their success and attributes for the purpose of prescribing delivery systems in a current or future project.

Design phase: A phase in the Handshaw Instructional Design Model in which the measurement strategy, instructional strategy, performance objectives, and implementation plans are created.

E-learning: Describes electronic delivery of tutorials, simulations, or games that provide instruction, with practice and feedback for learners. Sessions are usually conducted as asynchronous events because they can be done anytime without scheduling an instructor or class.

Electronic performance support systems (EPSS): Performance support that offers a more sophisticated range of options than a simple job aid, including audio and video interactivity and the option of hyperlinks to deliver more specific detail if needed.

Entry behaviors: Describe what a learner already knows about what is being taught in a defined learning event.

Evaluation: Using measured results to apply value or judgment to an outcome.

Field Test phase: A phase in the Handshaw Instructional Design Model in which the design team enlists a group of sample learners to test the complete solution in a controlled and structured session in order to record feedback and determine necessary revisions to the final solution.

Gaps Map: A needs analysis tool developed by Dana and Jim Robinson to identify gaps between current and required business needs and performance needs.

General characteristics: Describe the intended audience for a learning program in terms of their demographics.

Hierarchical task analysis: A step in the Learning Analysis phase of the Handshaw Instructional Design Model that documents the intellectual or knowledge-based tasks that are not directly observable but are inherent knowledge required to complete the task.

Implementation phase: A phase in the Handshaw Instructional Design Model in which the design team implements the training solution according to the prepared implementation plan and conducts any preplanned measurement of business impact and return on investment.

Implications for learning design: A key element to any learning analysis document in order to define the impact that analysis data should have on learning design.

Instructional design: A systematic approach to the design of instruction.

Job aid: A performance support tool that provides a reference for anything that eventually goes into memory as a result of repetitive use.

Learned capability: In performance objectives, the verb that describes the level of capability being learned.

Learner Tryout phase: A phase in the Handshaw Instructional Design Model in which the design team enlists sample learners to test a prototype in a controlled and structured session in order to record feedback and determine necessary revisions to the prototype and the overall measurement and instructional strategies.

Learning: The second level of the ROI Institute's five levels of measurement and evaluation, which "measures what participants learned in the program—information, knowledge, skills, and contacts (takeaways from the program)," as defined by the ROI Institute.

Learning Analysis phase: A phase in the Handshaw Instructional Design Model in which the designer, once training is identified as a possible solution to a performance and business goal, analyzes the task, audience, culture, and delivery systems as needed.

Learning culture analysis: An analysis of the learning culture of an organization for the purpose of identifying gaps between existing culture and desired culture in order to close the gaps and leverage culture as a theme or other element in instructional strategies.

Measurement: The act of observing something and scoring the results according to a predetermined scale.

Measurement strategy: The plan for measuring learner mastery of a learning solution based on required learner outcomes.

M-learning: Describes electronic delivery of learning or performance support content on mobile devices such as cell phones and tablets. Sessions are usually conducted as asynchronous events because they can be done anytime without scheduling an instructor or class.

Model: A "structure of symbols and operating rules which is supposed to match a set of relevant points in an existing structure or process," as defined by Karl Deutsch.

Needs/Gap Analysis phase: A phase in the Handshaw Instructional Design Model in which the designer meets with the true client to identify gaps in the business and performance outcomes by asking *should, is,* and *cause* questions in order to identify causal links and formulate possible solutions to achieve the stated business goal.

Needs hierarchy: A hierarchy of needs, which is essential to the consultant's understanding in order to analyze needs. The hierarchy includes business needs, performance needs, and capability and work environment needs.

Norm-referenced tests: Tests included in learning programs in which the performance levels represented by other learners' scores become the criteria for measuring learner mastery.

Object: In performance objectives, the object, or the "what," of the capability verb.

Performance consulting: A process in which clients and consultants partner to achieve the strategic outcome of enhancing workplace performance in support of business goals, as defined by Dana and Jim Robinson.

Performance improvement: Also called *human performance technology,* a process of selection, analysis, design, development, implementation, and evaluation of programs to most cost-effectively influence human behavior and accomplishment, as defined by the International Society for Performance Improvement (ISPI).

Performance need: Describes the performance that your workforce needs to accomplish in order to achieve a stated business goal.

Performance objectives: Written statements, derived from a task analysis, that provide an advanced organizer for learners, a contract for the entire design team to describe required outcomes, and a tool for designing measurement strategies and learner tests.

Performance support: An essential tool to help learners transfer learning into actual on-the-job performance.

Posttest: A test measuring learner mastery of the performance objectives of a course for the purpose of measuring final learner mastery.

Predictive validity: Describes whether the outcome of a test will predict the performance of the learner on the job.

Prescriptive feedback: In e-learning, written, audio, or video feedback to a learner in response to an answer or other action by the learner. This type of feedback is done to inform or instruct.

Pretest: A test measuring learner mastery of the performance objectives of a course for the purpose of diagnosis and prescription. A pretest can help determine individual learning needs.

Proactive Performance Consulting phase: A phase in the Handshaw Instructional Design Model in which the designer initiates a series of regular meetings with clients to inquire about the status of the business and identify business goals.

Procedural task analysis: A step in the Learning Analysis phase of the Handshaw Instructional Design Model that documents the observable behaviors needed to complete a task.

Production phase: A phase in the Handshaw Instructional Design Model in which the design team uses the analysis and design documents and a detailed content outline to produce all the required instructional and measurement instruments for the solution.

Prototype phase: A phase in the Handshaw Instructional Design Model in which the design team develops a prototype that represents the measurement and instructional strategies that you and your team agreed upon during the blueprint meeting.

Reaction: The first level of the ROI Institute's five levels of measurement and evaluation, which "measures reaction to, and satisfaction with, the experience, contents, and value of the program," as defined by the ROI Institute.

Reactive Performance Consulting phase: A phase in the Handshaw Instructional Design Model in which the designer responds to training requests by linking the training request to a business goal and uses structured questioning techniques to define desired outcomes.

Reframing meeting: A client meeting used to assess a client request through structured questioning to determine the appropriate level of analysis that will lead to clear and measurable business results. To accomplish this, you may need to get your client to view his or her request from a different point of view.

Reliability: Describes the consistency with which a test question measures learner mastery across a wide sampling of learners.

Responsive design: A software development technique that helps solve the problem of different screen sizes while delivering learning among mobile devices. The tool was originally designed to help websites provide an optimal viewing experience and has been adapted for use with m-learning.

Return on investment (ROI): The fifth level of the ROI Institute's five levels of measurement and evaluation, which "compares the monetary benefits of the business impact to the costs of the program," as defined by the ROI Institute.

Situation: In performance objectives, the stimulus for performing the task.

Social presence: A technique that can approximate the types of intergroup communication that takes place in a face-to-face classroom. It also creates a similar awareness of other individuals in an online virtual classroom.

Solution jumping: The practice of arriving at a solution prematurely without collecting data and identifying causal links to identify the real cause of a gap or problem.

Subject matter experts (SMEs): Members of the design team who work with the instructional designer to provide content and ensure that training programs are complete and accurate.

Task analysis: A step in the Learning Analysis phase of the Handshaw Instructional Design Model in which the required task is diagrammed to show a "snapshot of the perfect performer doing the task."

Teachable moment: In e-learning, the teachable moment comes from the point at which a learner makes a mistake in a simulation, or picks the wrong answer to a challenging question, and is presented with a hint or feedback.

Tools/constraints: In performance objectives, a description of the specific tools or methods that must be used to perform the task and any constraints such as time or required mastery.

True client: The owner of the line of business that is experiencing a performance problem. This person knows the current business goal, the internal and external barriers, and the strongest and weakest performers. He or she can make the decisions that will ultimately affect the final business results.

Validity: Describes whether a test measures the content or objectives that the test is intended to measure.

Virtual classroom: One of many terms that describe a synchronous learning event in which learners in diverse locations take part in a live classroom experience online, through the use of text, graphics, and/or video and audio delivered on their computers.

Web-based training: A synonym for e-learning, which describes electronic delivery of tutorials, simulations, or games that provide instruction with practice and feedback for learners. Sessions are usually conducted as asynchronous events because they can be done anytime without scheduling an instructor or class.

References and Resources

REFERENCES

Dick, Walter, and Lou Carey. *The Systematic Design of Instruction,* 4th edition. New York: HarperCollins, 1996.

Gagné, Robert M. *The Conditions of Learning and Theory of Instruction,* 4th edition. New York: CBS College Publishing, 1985.

Gery, Gloria. *Electronic Performance Support Systems.* Boston: Weingarten Publications, 1991.

Green, John A. *Teacher-Made Tests.* New York: Harper & Row, 1963.

LaBonte, Thomas J. *Building a New Performance Vision.* Alexandria, VA: American Society for Training & Development, 2001.

Molenda, Michael J., and Alan Januszewski. *Instructional Technology: A Definition with Commentary.* New York and London: Taylor & Francis Group, 2008.

Phillips, Patti P., and Jack J. Phillips. *The Consultant's Scorecard: Tracking ROI and Bottom-Line Impact of Consulting Projects,* 2nd edition. New York: McGraw-Hill, 2011.

Robinson, Dana G., and James C. Robinson. *Performance Consulting: A Practical Guide for HR and Learning Professionals,* 2nd edition. San Francisco: Berrett-Koehler, 2008.

Stake, Robert E. *Standards-Based and Responsive Evaluation.* Los Angeles: SAGE Publications, 2004.

Stolovitch, Harold D., and Erica J. Keeps. *Telling Ain't Training,* 2nd edition. Alexandria, VA: American Society for Training & Development, 2011.

PROFESSIONAL ORGANIZATIONS

American Society for Training and Development (ASTD)
1640 King Street, Box 1443
Alexandria, VA 22313–1443 USA
Phone: 1–800–628–2783 or 1–703–683–8100
Fax: 1–703–683–1523
Email: customercare@astd.org
Web: www.astd.org

International Society for Performance Improvement (ISPI)
P.O. Box 13035
Silver Spring, MD 20910 USA
Phone: 1–301–587–8570
Fax: 1–301–587–8573
Web: www.ispi.org

Society for Human Resource Management (SHRM)
1800 Duke Street
Alexandria, VA 22314 USA
Phone U.S. Only: 800–283-SHRM (7476)
Phone International: +1–703–548–3440
Fax: +1–703–535–6490
Web: www.shrm.org

Index

Selected Titles from the American Society for Training & Development (ASTD)

About the Author

DICK HANDSHAW, president of Handshaw, Inc., is a consultant speaker, and pioneer in the field, with more than 35 years of experience as a learning and performance improvement professional. He lives in Charlotte, North Carolina.